Islamic Political Ideology

By

Dr. Mohd. Zakirullah

Lulu Press Inc.
3101 Hillsborough St.
Raleigh, NC 27607
United States

First Edition (e format): 2015
ISBN: 978-1-312-33109-9
Second edition (Hard Core): 2015
ISBN: 978-1-312-48906-6

Published
by
Lulu Press Inc.
3101 Hillsborough St.
Raleigh, NC 27607
United States
www.lulu.com

Dedicated
To
My Childhood Friend
Khwaja Mushtaq Uddeen

Content

Introduction

Political Islam, now a days, has been a buzzword. Those days are by gone when Islam had to be taken as a collection of some believes and few specific rituals. Now, every one become aware, thanks to immense contribution of personalities like Islameel Shahaeed, Ahmed Shaheed, Maulana Mahmood ul Hasan, Mohammad Abduhu, Afghani, Iqbal, Hasan Al Banna, Maududi, Khumaeni, about the fact that Islam is a complete system of life, that includes social, economic, as well as Political matters.

After 9/11 there has been a flood of books related, directly or indirectly, to the political aspect of Islam. However, most of them were written from negative perspective and even aimed to project Islam as a religion that nurtures terrorism. However, there are works from pro-Islam writers, such as Azeez Ahmed, M. M. Shareef, Asghar Ali Engineer from India too; these works concentrate upon the political opinions, views, ideologies, philosophies presented by Muslim philosophers or writers. Generally, they start from Al Farabi, and going through Al Mawardi, Nizam ul Mulk Tusi, Al Ghazali, Ibn Jama'a, Ibn Baja, Ibn Taymia, Ibn Khalladun etc., and end up with one or the other Muslim thinker of the Modern days such as Afghani, Iqbal, Abduhu, Al Banna, Sanousi, Maududi or Khomeni. They intentionally or intentionally avoid the fundamental sources of the Islam. It might be out of their purview as some works such as M.M.Sharief's very title is Muslim political philosophy, not Islamic and Azeez Ahmed was dealing with tendencies and movements prevailed in India in a particular era, not ideal Islamic political frame work or theory. However, A.A. Maududi in his *Tafheem ul Quran, Khilafat wa Mulookiat, Islami Riyasat, Siyasi*

Kashmakash and some other treatises in Urdu language approached the fundamental sources of Islam directly and tried to deduce the Islamic, not Muslim, political theory based upon Quran and Sunna. There may be some other works in other regions of the world but the author has been limited his purview only to Indian sub-continent.

This work is primarily based upon the above sources and compiled to present the ideal Islamic political theory to the non-Urdu knowing readers of Indian sub-continent, that includes Pakistan and Bangladesh.

In the first chapter, attempt has been made to present the political theory as present in the Holy Quran. The second chapter, that is very much short due to its nature, deals with the Islamic state of the Prophetic era.

The third chapter gives a sketch of 'the Islamic polity in working' during the days of four pious caliphs. The fourth chapter provides an insight into the transformation of the Ideal Islamic form of Government into the hierarchical Monarchy. This scheme of chapters has been taken from Khilafat wa Mulokiat as it seems to be the most natural one.

The fifth chapter deals with the political theories and opinions prevalent among Muslims after the termination of the righteous era. Almost all the important Muslim philosophers were covered.

The sixth chapter looks into the socio-economic and political theories presented by various ulama and Muslims intelectuals during the British Colonialism in the Indian Sub-continent. The scope of the chapter is limited to the India-Pakistan, hence, many important Islamic organisations and significant personalities worthy to mention, such as Al Banna and Ikhwan, Sanousi and his Movement etc., could not find place here. Azeez Ahmed and M. M. Shareef, apart from some other sources including Maududi, has been the main source in this chapter. An analytical conclusion has been added to this compilation.

The very aim of the work is to provide an insight into the Islamic Political theory in English language as the majority of the Indian readers are not akin with Urdu language. Author is indebted to all those whose works has been utilised or referred in this work.

Date : 04-07-2015 **Dr. Mohd. Zakirullah**

Ch: I.
Political Theory in Quran

Islamic political theory lays its foundations in the Holy Quran. The Holy Scipture provides the conceptual and theoretical basis of the Islamic polity and outlines of the Islamic form of government. The political theory, enunciated in Quran, is primarily based upon the concept of Divine Sovereignty and Collective Vicegerency of Muslim community, which distinguishes it from other political theories.

However, it is an undeniable fact that the Quran did not present any obvious form of Islamic government or state. In fact, there are certain injunctions pertaining to the polity and government, that are quit enough to draw the outlines of the Islamic state and provide the basis to the political theory. For instance, the origin of the state can be traced to the Quranic injunction ' O ye who believe! Obey Allah, and obey the Messenger, and those charged with authority among you. (4:59), and there are numerous instructions concerning civil and penal codification that necessitate the establishment of a state under the Divine guidance.[1] Hence, the orthodox school

---

[1] As to the thief, male or female, cut off his or her hands: a punishment by way of example, from Allah, for their crime: and Allah is Exalted in Power. Full of Wisdom. (5:38);

O ye who believe! The law of equality is prescribed to you in cases of murder: the free for the free, the slave for the slave, the woman for the woman. But if the brother of the slain makes any remission, then grant any reasonable demand, and compensate him with handsome gratitude. This is a concession and a Mercy from your Lord. After this, whoever exceeds the limits shall be in grave penalty.(2:178);

And those who launch a charge against chaste women, and

trace the roots of the state to the *Al Samm*, that consists of *Quran, Sunnah* and *Ijam'a*, and not to the Quran alone.

Divine Sovereignty (Hakimiyyat-e-Ilahia)

The Islamic political theory is based upon, as mentioned above, the concept of Divine Sovereignty. Quran mentioned in unequivocal words that the Sovereignty rests only with Almighty and no other person or the institution enjoys any share in it, not even the state. In fact, the basic attribute of the Islamic State is that it lacks sovereignty on it its part; it is a mere vicegerent of Almighty on the earth to uphold His commands.

Quran mentioned the reason and justified Divine claim for Sovereignty on the basis that He is the Creator of the universe;[2] Hence all the power and governing authority lies with Him alone.[3]

---

produce not four witnesses, (to support their allegations), flog them with eighty stripes; and reject their evidence ever after: for such men are wicked transgressors;(4:4)

2 Verily His are the creation and command. (7: 54);

Say: Allah is the creator of the all things (13: 16);

He is the creator of the entire universe. (29: 63)

3 The command is for none but Allah's. (12: 40);

The command rests with none but Allah. He declares the truth and He is the best of judges. (6: 57);

He directs the affairs from the heavens. (32: 5);

knowest thou not that to Allah belongeth the dominion of the heavens and the earth? Besides Him, ye have neither patron nor helper. (2:252);

He to Whom belongs the dominion of the heavens and the earth: no son has He begotten, nor has He a partner in His dominion: it is He Who created all things, and ordered them in due proportions. (25: 2);

Say: "To whom belong the earth and all beings therein? (Say) if ye know!"(23: 83);

He possesses every right to seek the unconditional obedience and loyalty from His own creatures.[4]

Another basis for His sovereignty is the human beings own agreement with the Almighty on the *Yaom-e-alast* i.e. the day of agreement. Quran claims that Almighty drew the souls of all the human beings and made them testify. All they said that they would obey and worship Him.[5] Then the Almighty inculcate this oath or agreement in their consciousness and very nature. Hence, regarding any other entity as their sovereign amounts to the breach of the contract that is inherent in their instinct. This is so inherent in human nature that the non-believers and polytheists too did not deny the existence of the God, nor that the whole mechanism of universe is functioning in accordance with His commands.[6]

Say: "Who is the Lord of the seven heavens, and the Lord of the Throne (of Glory) Supreme?" (23: 86);

Say:"Who is it in whose hands is the governance of all things, who protects (all), but is not protected (of any)? (Say) if ye know.(23: 88)

4 If Allah touch thee with affliction, none can remove it but He; if He touch thee with happiness, He hath power over all things." He is the Irresistible, (watching) from above over His worshippers; and He is the Wise, Acquainted with all things. (6: 16);

For Allah is He Who gives (all) Sustenance, - Lord of Power - steadfast (forever). (51: 58)

5 When thy Lord drew forth from the Children of Adam from their loins, their descendants, and made them testify concerning themselves, (saying): "Am I not your Lord (Who cherishes and sustains you)?" They said: "Yea! We do testify!" (This), lest ye should say on the Day of Judgement: "Of this we were never mindful". (7: 172)

6 If thou ask them, Who created them, they will certainly say, Allah: how then are they deluded away (from the Truth)? (43: 87);

Say: "Who is it that sustains you (in life) from the sky and from the earth? Or who is it that has power over hearing and sight? And who is

The Quranic concepts of the Omnipotence of God and the Divine Sovereignty are so vitally intertwined that the negation of one amounts the negation of the other *ipso facto*.[7]

Holy Quran declares in unequivocal words that Almighty is the Omnipotent, Omnipresent, Omniscient, Irresistible and Supreme; His powers are universal and comprehensive; They are absolute and inalienable to Him; He did not have any counterpart in His powers, nor even wife or children.[8] These claims are so-politically

---

it that brings out the living from the dead and the dead from the living? And who is it that rules and regulates all affairs?" They will soon say, "Allah". Say, "Will ye not then show piety (to Him)?" (10: 31)

7 He to Whom belongs the dominion of the heavens and the earth: no son has He begotten, nor has He a partner in His dominion: it is He Who created all things, and ordered them in due proportions. (25: 2);

Say: "Allah knows best how long they stayed: with Him is (the knowledge of) the secrets of the heavens and the earth: how clearly He sees, how finely He hears (everything)! They have no protector other than Him; nor does He share His Command with any person whatsoever. (18: 26)

8 Allah is He, than Whom there is no other god; the Sovereign, the Holy One, the Source of Peace (and Perfection), the Guardian of Faith, the Preserver of Safety, the Exalted in Might, the Irresistible, the Supreme: Glory to Allah! (High is He) above the partners they attribute to Him. (59: 23);

Whatever is in the heavens and on earth, doth declare the Praises and Glory of Allah; the Sovereign, the Holy One, the Exalted in Might, the Wise. (62: 1)

Yet there are men who take (for worship) others besides Allah, as equal (with Allah): they love them as they should love Allah, but those of Faith are overflowing in their love for Allah. If only the unrighteous could see, behold, they would see the Punishment: that to Allah belongs all power, and Allah will strongly enforce the Punishment. (2: 165);

Say: if there had been (other) gods with Him, - as they say -

oriented that it would be difficult to limit them to the religious arena.[9] By observing them an impartial analyst can conclude that the Quran obviously commands its believers to establish the rule of the God over the earth. However, in the physical sphere of the Universe His sovereignty is established by coercion over the each and every object including the Man; he, like other objects, is subject to His Will without any choice; but in the social and political sphere man is physically, not morally, free for acceptance or rejection of his sovereignty. He would be kind enough to remind the men, through His prophets, of their agreement with Him, as the rejection cause unending punishment in their eternal life.

---

behold, they would certainly have sought out a way to the Lord of the Throne! Glory to Him! He is high above all that they say! Exalted and Great (beyond measure)! (17: 42-43);

Say: "Do ye see what it is ye invoke besides Allah? Show me what it is they have created on earth, or have they a share in the heavens? Bring me a Book (revealed) before this, or any remnant of knowledge (ye may have), if ye are telling the truth!" (46: 4-5);

To Him is due the primal origin of the heavens and the earth: how can He have a son when He hath no consort? He created all things, and He hath full knowledge of all things. That is Allah, your Lord! There is no god but He, the Creator of all things; then worship ye Him; and He hath power to dispose of all affairs. (6: 101-102);

He to Whom belongs the dominion of the heavens and the earth: no son has He begotten, nor has He a partner in His dominion: it is He Who created all things, and ordered them in due proportions. Yet have they taken, besides Him, gods that can create nothing but are themselves created; that have no control of hurt or good to themselves; nor can they control Death nor Life nor Resurrection. (25: 2-3)

[9] Allah has said: "Take not (for worship) two gods: for He is just One God: then fear Me (and Me alone)." (16: 51)

Divine Law (Shariah)

The Quran is the supreme law or constitutional framework for the Islamic State since it contains the manifested Will of the Almighty.[10] But it is obvious that no book could contain all the laws required for a living society. Hence, in the form of Sunnah, i.e. the words and practices of His Prophet, He provides a living source of law to the Islamic State. In other words, the prophet is embodiment of the legal sovereignty of Almighty. Holy Quran gives obvious injunctions in this regard.[11]

---

10 This is the book; in it is guidance, sure, without doubt, to those who fear Allah; (2: 2);

To thee we sent the scripture that came before it, and guiding in safety. So judge between them by what Allah hath revealed and follow not their vain desires, diverging from the truth what hath come to thee. To each among you, we prescribed a law and open way. (5: 48)

11 We sent not a Messenger, but to be obeyed, in accordance with the Will of Allah. If they had only, when they were unjust to themselves, come unto thee and asked Allah's forgiveness, and the Messenger had asked forgiveness for them, they would have found Allah indeed Oft-Returning, Most Merciful. (4: 65);

He who obeys the Messenger, obeys Allah; but if any turn away, We have not sent thee to watch over their (evil deeds). (4: 80)

Then We put thee on the (right) Way of Religion: so follow thou that (Way), and follow not the desires of those who know not. (45: 18);

If anyone contends with the Messenger even after guidance has been plainly conveyed to him, and follows a path other than that becoming to men of Faith, We shall leave him in the path he has chosen, and land him in Hell, what an evil refuge! (4: 115);

What Allah has bestowed on His Messenger (and taken away) from the people of the townships, belongs to Allah, to His Messenger and to kindred and orphans, the needy and the wayfarer; in order that it may not (merely) make a circuit between the wealthy among you. So take

The people and their emir are bound to deduce laws from the *Quran* and the *Sunnah.* If in a particular situation they could not find any law in these sources then they can resort to *Shura* and *Ijm'a* i.e. consultation and consensus. They do not enjoy absolute powers to legislate; they are bound to work within the limits laid down by the *shariah.*[12]

Collective Vicegerency (Khilafat-e-Ummah)

In the Islamic State, the Vicegerency is not vested in anyone or few individuals, but, according to the Quran, in the Muslim community *(Ummate Muslimah)* as a whole. Quran declares in unambiguous words that:

'Allah has promised, to those among you who

---

what the Messenger assigns to you, and deny yourselves that which he withholds from you. And fear Allah; for Allah is strict in Punishment. (59: 7)

[12] Behold, thy Lord said to the angels: "I will create a vicegerent on earth". They said: "Wilt Thou place therein one who will make mischief therein and shed blood? Whilst we do celebrate Thy praise and glorify Thy holy (name)?" He said: "I know what ye know not". (2: 30);

He it is that has made you inheritors in the earth: if, then, any do reject (Allah), their rejection (works) against themselves: their rejection but adds to the odium for the Unbelievers in the sight of their Lord: their rejection but adds to (their own) undoing. (35: 39);

Allah has promised, to those among you who believe and work righteous deeds, that He will, of a surety, grant them in the land, inheritance (of power), as He granted it to those before them; that He will establish in authority their religion, the one which He has chosen for them; and that He will change (their state), after the fear in which they (lived), to one of security and peace: `They will worship Me (alone) and not associate aught with Me.' If any do reject Faith after this, they are rebellious and wicked. (24: 55)

> believe and work righteous deeds, that He will, of a surety, grant them in the land, inheritance (of power), as He granted it to those before them; that He will establish in authority their religion, the one which He has chosen for them; and that He will change (their state), after the fear in which they (lived), to one of security and peace: 'They will worship Me (alone) and not associate aught with Me.' If any do reject Faith after this, they are rebellious and wicked. (24: 55)

All those who possess faith in the tenets of Islam and follow them in practice are the members of the Vicegerency. Politically speaking, all those who surrendered their free will to the Will of Almighty and accepted His sovereignty over themselves in all manifestations, including political, of their volitional life, deliberately as well as practically, are collectively His vicegerents. Being vicegerents they are bound to follow and enforce the Will of their Master, revealed to them through His prophet in the shape of Quran and Sunnah, practices of the prophet himself, over the earth. They are not authorised or empowered, even by common concurrence, to make any alteration, addition or deletion to His and His prophet's commandments.[13]

Vicegerent (Khilafah)

The Vicegerency, although, rests with the *Ummah* as a whole, but in practice it is difficult to enforce it collectively. Hence, the *ummah* have to adopt an emir i.e. leader to lead them in the enforcement of His Will. The institution of the Caliph owes its

---

13 The command is none for Allah's (12: 40);
All the affairs go back to Allah (54: 5);
These are the limits ordained by Allah. So, do not transgress them (2:219)

existence to the certain Quranic injunctions such as:

'Then We made you heirs in the land after them, to see how ye would behave! (10: 14);

O David! We did indeed make thee a vicegerent on earth: so judge thou between men in Truth (and justice): nor follow thou the lusts (of thy heart), for they will mislead thee from the Path of Allah: for those who wander astray from the Path of Allah, is a Penalty Grievous, for that they forget the Day of Account.(38:26)

'Behold, thy Lord said to the angels: "I will create a vicegerent on earth". (2: 30).

However, there are no deliberate injunctions, in Quran, regarding the procedure to establish the Amir but the very concept of collective Vicegerency implies that the leader of the vicegerents should be adopted with the consent of all the vicegerents, i.e., believers. Since all members of *ummah* shared the Vicegerency equally, if there is necessity to represent these numerous members of Vicegerency by one person it is rational that he should be elected unanimously, or atlas with majority of them. The general spirit of Quran is also in favour of a democratic method as it condemns becoming representative of anyone by coercion.[14]

Investiture to Amir *(Ba'et)*

The Holy Book left the matter and procedure of election of the Amir to the discretion of the Muslim community that it would adopt appropriate procedure according to the conditions and circumstances prevailing at that time. However, the Quran instructed the prophet to take the *ba'et* whenever some one came to

---

[14] Those who hearken to their Lord, and establish regular prayer; who (conduct) their affairs by mutual Consultation; who spend out of what We bestow on them for Sustenance; (42: 38)

do so and have a positive reference to the *Ba'ete Rizwan* as an appropriate method to render the allegiance to an emir.[15] The *Ba'ete Rizwan* was rather an oath of political and military significance as all these persons already had a religious oath that they regard the Almighty as only God and the prophet Muhammad as His last messenger. The second oath was to render temporal obedience to fight under the command of the Prophet Muhammad against the Meccan people.

Concept of *Ba'et* includes a strong sense of contract between the ruler and the ruled. It will be an oath of conditional obedience that if the ruler provide the security to life and property of the individual and enforce the Divine law he will obey him and his orders.

Consultation *(Shura)*

The *Ameer* of the Muslim *Ummah* will not be an absolute and autocratic ruler. The Quranic injunction "who (conduct) their affairs by mutual consultation" binds him to conduct the affairs of

---

15 O Prophet! When believing women come to thee to take the oath of fealty to thee, that they will not associate in worship any other thing whatever with Allah, that they will not steal, that they will not commit adultery (or fornication), that they will not kill their children, that they will not utter slander, intentionally forging falsehood, and that they will not disobey thee in any just matter; then do thou receive their fealty, and pray to Allah for the forgiveness (of their sins): for Allah is Oft-Forgiving, Most Merciful.(60 : 12);

Verily those who plight their fealty to thee do no less than plight their fealty to Allah: the Hand of Allah is over their hands: then anyone who violates his oath, does so to the harm of his own soul, and anyone who fulfils what he has covenanted with Allah, Allah will soon grant him a great Reward.(48 : 10)

the state by mutual consultation with the Muslims or the learned men among them.[16] There is difference of opinion among the jurists that whether this consultation should be only with the *as hab hall wo 'aqd or* with all the Muslims in general, and whether it is obligatory on the part of the ruler to have an established *shura,* i.e., consultative council or not, since the Quranic injunctions in this regard are vague.

Revolt (Khuruj)

Quran prescribes the limits to the authority of the state over citizens and obedience from citizens to the state. According to the Quranic provisions the state should exercise its authority in conformity with *shari'a,* the Divine laws and the citizens should obey only those laws and orders of the authorities which are in accordance with the Divine laws, as revealed in Quran and Sunnah.[17] The origin of the very concept of *Khuruj* in Islam can be traced to the Quranic provisions given in *Surah* 5, *Ayah* 2, and *Surah* 76, *Ayah* 24,

Help ye one another in righteousness and piety; but

---

[16] Those who hearken to their Lord, and establish regular prayer; who (conduct) their affairs by mutual Consultation; who spend out of what We bestow on them for Sustenance; (42: 38)

[17] Help ye one another in righteousness and piety; but help ye not one another in sin rancour (5: 2);

We sent not a Messenger, but to be obeyed, in accordance with the Will of Allah. If they had only, when they were unjust to themselves, come unto thee and asked Allah's forgiveness, and the Messenger had asked forgiveness for them, they would have found Allah indeed Oft-Returning, Most Merciful. (4: 64);

Therefore be patient with constancy to the Command of thy Lord, and hearken not to the sinner or the ingrate among them. (76: 24)

> help ye not one another in sin rancour. (5: 2);
>
> Therefore be patient with constancy to the Command of thy Lord, and hearken not to the sinner or the ingrate among them. (76: 24)

These Quranic provisions clearly state that there should be no obedience against the orders of Allah and His Apostle; and this implies to resist and revolt *(khuruj)* against such authorities.[18] Moreover, the very concept of *Ba'et* involves the *khuruj* since it is conditional. The caliph, by the words of investiture, binds himself to the believers that he will fulfil his duties according to the *Shari'a* and receive their obedience in exchange. Quran instructs the prophet to take the *ba'et* with the condition that:

> O Prophet! When believing women come to thee to take the oath of fealty to thee, that they will not associate in worship any other thing whatever with Allah, that they will not steal, that they will not commit adultery (or fornication), that they will not kill their children, that they will not utter slander, intentionally forging falsehood, and that they will not disobey thee in any just matter; then do thou receive their fealty, and pray to Allah for the forgiveness (of their sins): for Allah is Oft-Forgiving,

---

[18] Therefore be patient with constancy to the Command of thy Lord, and hearken not to the sinner or the ingrate among them. (76: 24);

Help ye one another in righteousness and piety; but help ye not one another in sin rancour (5: 2);

O Prophet! When believing women come to thee to take the oath of fealty to thee, that they will not associate in worship any other thing whatever with Allah, that they will not steal, that they will not commit adultery (or fornication), that they will not kill their children, that they will not utter slander, intentionally forging falsehood, and that they will not disobey thee in any just matter; then do thou receive their fealty, and pray to Allah for the forgiveness (of their sins): for Allah is Oft-Forgiving, Most Merciful.(60 : 12);

Most Merciful.(60 : 12);

Hence, transgression of *shari'a* by the caliph amounts to the violation of the contract on the part of caliph, and, thereby, release the other party of the contract, the believers, also from the *ba'et*. In other words, if the caliph violates the *shari'a,* the people can revolt against him. However, the transgression of the *shari'a* by the state authorities must be obvious and clear to revolt against them. Otherwise, the citizens are bound to follow the state-orders, since there will be chaos if the citizens deny the state authority indiscriminately.[19] Quran warn stern action against those who disturb the order in society and create chaos.[20]

Ummah

The Islamic concept of *Ummah* is different from, in fact, the

---

[19] O ye who believe! Obey Allah, and obey the Messenger, and those charged with authority among you. If ye differ in anything among yourselves, refer it to Allah and His Messenger, if ye do believe in Allah and the Last Day: that is best, and most suitable for final determination. (4: 59)

[20] To the Madyan people We sent Shu'aib, one of their own brethren: he said: "O my people! Worship Allah; ye have no other god but Him. Now hat come unto you a Clear (Sign) from your Lord! Give just measure and weight, nor withhold from the people the things that are their due; and do no mischief on the earth after it has been set in order: that will be best for you, if ye have Faith. (7: 85);

For tumult and oppression are worse than slaughter; (2: 191);

The punishment of those who wage war against Allah and His Messenger, and strive with might and main for mischief through the land is: execution, or crucifixion, or the cutting off of hands and feet from opposite sides, or exile from the land: that is their disgrace in this world, and a heavy punishment is theirs in the Hereafter; (5: 33)

negation of, the modern concept of nationalism. The European Nationalism is based upon the racial, linguistic, geographical, political and other such elements. Islamic *Ummah*, contrary to this, transcends family, clan, race, language, geographical affiliation and all such irrational elements and engulf all the like-minded people, those who believe in Omnipotence of God Almighty and ultimacy of the prophethood of Muhammad, of the entire world to form an entity. Faith is the basic cohesive and the only unifying factor amidst the diversity of racial, linguistic, geographical factors. It is based upon the fraternity of creed. Quran declares that all the members of the *Ummah* are brethren and equal in matters of status and dignity. Moreover, they enjoy equal social and political powers.

According to Quran the clans or the tribes are only to identify the persons and not to discriminate among them. If there would be any honour, preference or superiority that would be based on one's deeds and piousness, not on descent.[21]

Another characteristic feature of the Islamic Ummah is that it is not a segregated and closed entity; any one at any time can join it by mere witnessing from his heart and pronouncing with tongue that there is no God save Allah and Muhammad is the Prophet.

Moreover, this Ummah is a congregation with a certain purpose, that is *Amr bil m'aroof and Nahi 'anil munkar,* to enjoin the righteousness and to prevent the misdeeds among the humanity. Quran reads:

"Thus, have We made of you an Ummat justly

---

[21] O mankind! We created you from a single (pair) of a male and a female, and made you into nations and tribes, that ye may know each other (not that ye may despise each other). Verily the most honoured of you in the sight of Allah is (he who is) the most righteous of you. And Allah has full Knowledge and is well acquainted (with all things).(49: 13)

balanced, that ye might be witnesses over the nations and the Messenger a witness over yourselves?" (2: 143)

"Ye are the best of Peoples, evolved for humankind, enjoining what is right, forbidding what is wrong, and believing in Allah. If only the People of the Book had Faith, it were best for them; among them are some that have Faith, but most of them are perverted transgressors."(3: 110)

For achieving this purpose they should preach the true creed among the non-believers peacefully and seek the establishment of the God's Will on the entire earth through *Jihad,* that is a war against those who are in authority and not permitting their subjects to follow the God's ordain. But certainly it would not be a preaching-through sword or conversion by coercion, since, after subjugating such evil authority and establishment of God's Will, each and every one will be allowed to follow his own religion according to his own choice. Quran clearly states that ' there will be no compulsion in religion '(2: 256). In fact, this war is to remove the constrains on the free will of those who wish to surrender themselves to the God and to become a part of the Islamic Ummah. Quran says:

And fight them on until there is no more tumult or oppression, and there prevails justice and faith in Allah altogether and everywhere; but if they cease, verily Allah doth see all that they do. (8: 39)

If they succeed in doing so, they are the true vicegerents of the God on earth:

Allah has promised, to those among you who believe and work righteous deeds, that He will, of a surety, grant them in the land, inheritance (of power), as He granted it to those before them; that He will establish in authority their religion, the one which He has chosen for them; and that He will change (their state), after the fear in which they (lived), to one of security and peace: `They will worship Me (alone) and not associate aught with Me.' If any do reject Faith after this, they are rebellious and wicked.(24 : 59)

Justice ('Adl)

Quran insist that the God Almighty is *'Adil,* the Justice and He adores the *'Adl,* the just, and hate the injustice. All His acts and commands are bound to be just since He won't do injustice; the universe is based upon the justice and He established the justice in the physical and natural spheres of the universe and instructs the mankind to be just and establish justice in their volitional life. Certain acts of Him may be appeared as unjust to us but that is only because the limitedness of our wisdom.

> Allah commands justice, the doing of good, and liberality to kith and kin, and He forbids all shameful deeds, and injustice and rebellion; He instructs you, that ye may receive admonition. (16: 90)

Being the Justice and the very creator of the Just he knows very well that what is just and what is not; hence, justice in volitional life is possible only when His commands are enforced in full; the man can render justice but can not form the basic principles of justice as his ration is limited, fallible and partial and there will be no justice if it is rendered on the basis of man-made principles. In brief, the justice implied only in the enforcement of the commandments of God Almighty in all spheres of life.

Quran instructs, hundreds of time, its followers to be just in their private life as well establish justice in public life.[22] Moreover,

---

[22] And come not nigh to the orphan's property, except to improve it, until he attains the age of full strength; give measure and weight with (full) justice; no burden do We place on any soul, but that which it can bear, whenever ye speak, speak justly, even if a near relative is

the justice in Islam involves, unlike the western concept of justice, that limit itself to the national boundaries and injustice in international matters termed as diplomacy, the national and international spheres equally. Quran instructs the Muslims and their authorities to be just in international realms and to be abiding by the covenants with other nations:

> Allah commands justice, the doing of good, and liberality to kith and kin, and He forbids all shameful deeds, and injustice and rebellion: He instructs you, that ye may receive admonition. (16; 90);
>
> Allah doth command you to render back your Trusts to those to whom they are due; and when ye judge between man and man, that ye judge with justice: verily how excellent is the teaching which He giveth you! For Allah is He Who heareth and seeth all things. (4:58);
>
> O ye who believe! Stand out firmly for justice, as witnesses to Allah, even as against yourselves, or your parents, or your kin, and whether it be (against) rich or poor: for Allah can best protect both. Follow not the lusts (of your hearts), lest ye swerve, and if ye distort (justice) or decline to do justice, verily Allah is well acquainted with all that ye do. (4: 135);
>
> O ye who believe! Stand out firmly for Allah, as witnesses to fair dealing, and let not the hatred of others to you make you swerve to wrong and depart from justice. Be just: that is next to Piety: and fear Allah. For

---

concerned; and fulfil the Covenant of Allah: thus doth He command you, that ye may remember. (6: 152);

If ye fear that ye shall not be able to deal justly with the orphans, marry women of your choice, two, or three, or four; but if ye fear that ye shall not be able to deal justly (with them), then only one, or (a captive) that your right hands possess. That will be more suitable, to prevent you from doing injustice. (4: 3)

Allah is well acquainted with all that ye do. (5: 8); [23]

Non-Muslim Subjects (Ahl-uz-Zimmah)

Islamic state will enter into an agreement with its non-believing citizens and through the agreement it will take the *Zimmah,* responsibility, of their life, liberty, property, and dignity,

---

[23] The word of thy Lord doth find its fulfilment in truth and in justice: none can change His Words for He is the One Who heareth and knoweth all. (6: 115);

Now then, for that (reason), call (them to the Faith), and stand steadfast as thou art commanded, nor follow thou their vain desires; but say: "I believe in the Book which Allah has sent down; and I am commanded to judge justly between you. Allah is our Lord and your Lord: for us (is the responsibility for) our deeds, and for you for your deeds, there is no contention between you and us. Allah will bring us together, and to Him is (our) final goal." (42: 15);

Him Who created thee, fashioned thee in due proportion, and gave thee a just bias; (82: 7);

And be not like a woman who breaks into untwisted strands the yarn she has spun after it has become strong. Nor take your oaths to practice deception between yourselves, lest one party should be more numerous than another: for Allah will test you by this; and on the Day of Judgement, He will certainly make clear to you (the truth of) that wherein ye disagree. (16: 92);

(But the treaties are) not dissolved with those Pagans with whom ye have entered into alliance and who have not subsequently failed you in aught, nor aided anyone against you. So fulfil your engagements with them to the end of their term: for Allah loveth the righteous.-------How can there be a league, before Allah and His Messenger, with the Pagans, except those with whom ye made a treaty near the Sacred Mosque? As long as these stand true to you, stand ye true to them: for Allah doth love the righteous. (9: 4 & 7)

in return of a tax namely *Jizya.* Hence, they called *Ahluz Zimmah* or *Zimmis* in short, the people under responsibility. Quran ordains that all matters pertaining to them will invariably be decided in accordance with the terms of the treaty or agreement. It enjoins that once the terms have been settled with any group or community, they must be fully adhered to, even if they seem to be distasteful later on.[24] Thus, in case of the contracted non-Muslims the fundamental principle is that the relations between them and the Islamic State shall be based on the terms of the agreement.[25] They are to be treated according to their religious injunctions regarding their personal affairs, viz., marriage, divorce, inheritance etc. In brief, the non-believers of an Islamic state enjoy the following rights:

1- Right to life: Quran guarantees the right to life to all citizens, irrespective of religion and sex. According Quranic provisions no one can be deprived of his life. God Almighty ordains:

> "Do not kill any soul whom God has forbidden you to, except through law."(17:33)

If any one will violate the provision it will invoke capital punishment in *Qisas*, retaliation. However, Quran empowers the state to sanction capital punishment in certain crimes, viz., Murder,[26] Apostasy,[27]and Armed resistance,[28] if allegation of any of

---

24 (But the treaties are) not dissolved with those pagans with whom Ye have entered into alliance and who have not subsequently failed you in aught nor aided anyone against you. So fulfil your engagements with them to the end of their term: for Allah loveth the righteous.(9:4)

25 As long as these(non-believers) stand true to you stand ye true to them: For Allah doth love the righteous.(9:7)

26 (We ordained there in for them) life for life, eye for eye.(5:45);
The free for free and slave for slave; and the female for the female.(2:175)

these crimes proved by due legal process.

2- Right to Privacy: Quran strictly prohibits encroachment upon the privacy of the citizens, Even the state authorities should not enquire in to the private affairs of the individuals unnecessarily. Quran ordains:

> "And spy not on each other, nor speak ill of each other behind their backs."(49:12)

3- Right to form Associations: Quran grants the right to form associations and organisations to all for righteous purpose. Quran suggests:

> "Let there arise out a band of people inviting to all that is good, enjoying what is right and forbidding what is wrong. They are one's to attain felicity." (3:104)

4- Right to Equality before Law: Quran regards the entire humanity as descendants of a single couple Adam and Eve. Hence, it disregards any sort of inequality on the basis of the birth, cast, race, language, colour, tribe etc. All the citizens, Muslims and non-Muslims of the Islamic State are equal before law. The blood of the non-Muslim citizens is as sacrosanct as that of Muslim citizen and his property is as inviolable as of Muslim. If a Muslim kills a non-Muslim citizen retribution and restitution will have to be made just as for killing a Muslim. Quran in unequivocal words ordains not to distinguish between man and man.

5- Right to Protection of Honour and Dignity: No one can be deprived of his honour and dignity for any reason. Quran instructs

---

[27] But if they violated their oaths after their covenants and taunt you for your faith, fight ye the chiefs of unfaith.(9:12)

[28] The penalty for those who wage war on God and His Messenger and spread havoc through the land is to be slaughtered or crucified or to have their hands and feet cut off on opposite sides or to banish from the land.(5:33)

the individual that they should not laugh or make fun of each other; nor they should defame nor be sarcastic to each other. The same provision applies to the state also:

> Ye who believe! Do not let one (set of) people make fun of another set; perhaps they are better than themselves .Nor let any (set of) women make fun of other women. Perhaps they are better than themselves. (49:11)

6- Right to Religious Tolerance: Quran guarantees the protection of the sanctity of the Holy personalities and places of worship of non-Muslims. Quran ordains:

> "Do not abuse those they appeal to instead of God, lest they abuse God out of enmity without realising it." (6:108)

Moreover, Quran gives the right to retain, practice, profess and inherit their religion to the non-believers. This implies the right to be treated in personal maters according to their personal law.

The Islamic State is obliged to respect and protect these rights. Generally, the non-believers do not share the political rights, while as they enjoy certain civil right, in addition to those enjoyed by the believers. Discrimination in this regard is the logical outcome and natural consequence of the theory of Divine sovereignty and ideological orientation of the Islamic State. In fact, rights in an Islamic state can be classified in three categories viz., Universal rights, exclusive rights of believers and exclusive rights of non-believers.

In addition to these rights, that are available to both Muslims and non-Muslims, the non-Muslims enjoy certain exclusive rights such as Right to change religion, freedom from the religious obligations of their own religion and freedom from taking part in military expeditions.

Foreign Policy:

Quran provides, even, the basic principles of foreign policy. These principles oriented the Islamic State towards equity and justice and not mere the national interests. Quran, in unequivocal words, condemns treachery on the name of the selfish or national interests:

> O ye who believe! Stand out firmly for Allah, as witnesses to fair dealing, and let not the hatred of others to you make you swerve to wrong and depart from justice. Be just: that is next to Piety; and fear Allah. For Allah is well acquainted with all that ye do. (5: 8)

These principles can be enumerated as follows:

1-Sanctity of the Treaties and Agreements: The Islamic state, according to the Quran, has to follow all her treaties and agreements as long as the other party respecting it. The Islamic State cannot deceit to or treason upon another state or nation. If dissolution of the treaty become necessary the other party is to be informed about that. There are specific Quranic injunctions in this regard:

> "As longs as these stand true to you, stand ye true to them, Of Allah doth love the righteous."(9:7)
>
> "If thou fearest treachery from any group, throw back (their covenants) to them on equal terms, For Allah loveth not the treacherous."
>
> "And fulfil agreements, for every agreement will be enquired into."(17:34)

2-Honesty and Truthfulness: The Islamic State never deceit or treason upon the others for any reason and interest. Quran ordains:

> "And not take your oaths to practise deception between your selves with them that some one's foot may slip after it was firmly planted, and ye may have to taste the evil of having hindered from the path of Allah.

(16:94)"

3- Reverence to international Justice: The Islamic State strives to promote justice among the nations. It won't ignore this principle even against her enemies. There is specific provision in the Quran in this regard:

> O ye who believe! Stand out firmly for justice, as witnesses to Allah, even as against yourselves, or your parents, or your kin, and whether it be (against) rich or poor: for Allah can best protect both. Follow not the lusts (of your hearts), lest ye swerve, and if ye distort (justice) or decline to do justice, verily Allah is well acquainted with all that ye do. (4: 135)

4- Respect for neutral: Th Islamic State has to pay due regard to the boundaries of the neutral countries or nations during war as well as peace. Quran instructs:

> "Except those who join a nation between whom and you there is a treaty, or those who approach you with hearts restraining them from fighting you or fighting their own people." (4:90)

5- Preference to the Reconciliation: the Islamic State rather prefers to reconciliation but not on the cost of principles or beliefs. Quran recommends:

> But if enemy incline towards peace, do thou incline peace and trust in Allah. (8:61)

6-Refraining from Mischief on Earth: Islamic State is not intended to seek dominance on the earth or to create mischief or chaos. It is aimed to establish the dominance of the almighty on earth:

> "That home here after we shall giveth to those who intend not dominance or mischief on earth."

7-Friendliness towards non-hostile nations: Islamic State is intended to wards friendly relations and harmony with other nations of the world. Quran decrees:

> "Allah forbids you not with regard to those who fight you not for (your) Faith nor drive you out of your homes from dealing kindly and justly with them: for Allah loveth those who are just. (60:8)

8-Fair Attitude with Fairmen: Islamic State has to deal fairly and kindly with those who are fair and honest in their dealings:

> "Is there any reward for good other than good."(55:60)

9- Proportionate Retaliation: Islamic State will not transgresses the limits in dealing with those who involved in oppression. Quran ordains:

> "There is the law of equality. If then anyone transgresses the prohibition against you transgress ye likewise against him. But fear Allah and know that Allah is with those who restrain themselves. (2:194)
>
> And if ye do catch them out catch them out no worse than they catch you out but if ye show patience that is indeed the best (course) for those who are patient. (16:126)
>
> The recompense for an injury is an injury equal thereto (in degree): but if a person forgives and makes reconciliation His reward is due from Allah: for (Allah) loveth not those who do wrong. (42:40)

10- Courageous Policy: Inclination towards peace, reconciliation, friendly attitude towards neutrals does not imply that the foreign policy of Islamic State should be one of the cowardice. The above mentioned ayah of surah eight implies that the Muslims should possess trust on Allah and accept the peace proposals of the enemies, but if they violate their covenant then Quran instructs:

> O Apostle! Rouse the believers to the fight. If there are twenty amongst you patient and persevering they will vanquish two hundred: if a hundred they will vanquish a thousand of the unbelievers: for these are a people

without understanding. (8:65)

Thus, Quran provides the spiritual basis and the theological foundations to the Islamic State. It is not only a Holy Book of a religious community but rather a constitution of the Islamic State also.

Ch. II.
The Islamic State during Prophet's Life

The Islamic State, virtually, came into vogue with the Prophet's arrival in Yathrib, latter renown as Madinath un Nabi, the Prophet's city. Although, neither the Prophet, nor the peoples of Yathrib deliberately formulated the state, nor established the prophet as ruler, the Yathrib in post-migration period developed all the essential characteristics of the state. In a short span of time, it became, for all practical purposes, a sovereign state having ties and mutual agreements with neighbouring friends and foes, even with the Meccan chieftains, and well defined boundaries. According to the traditions the prophet declared the Medinah as Harem, the city of peace, and instructed the Ka'abb bin Malik to eruct watching towers at the boundaries of the newly established state,[29] and concluded agreements with the tribes living in and around the Medina.[30] By these agreements all the tribes owes their allegiance to the prophet, although they did not accept his prophethood, but accredited his supremacy over themselves and given the power to

[29] The prophet instructed to eruct watching towers at *Zatul Jaish,* that was at the Hafirah Hills and at the centre of Ba'eda on the Mecca-Medina Highway, *Mashirab,* that is adjacent to *Zatul Jaish,* Mukhidh Hills, that is on the way to Syria, Hafya, that is north of Medina, *Zul 'Asheer,* that is on the edge of Hafya, and on the Taem Hills, that are east to *Medinah.* The area between these consists of One square *manzil. (*Hameedullah Siddiqui: *'Ahde Nabwi ke Maedane Jung* p 11- 12 - taken from Naeem Siddiqui: *Muhsine Insaniat*. p 412-413)

[30] Such as Banu Aus, Banu Khazraj, Banu Hamzah, Banu Juahaena, Banu Dhumarah, Banu Zur'a, Banu Arrab'a and Banu Mudlij.(Ibid, taken from Naeem Siddiqui: *Muhsine Insaniat*. P. 364)

regulate their civil affairs and to settle their disputes. Prophet occasionally sent patrolling parties to protect the boundaries of the state; he appointed Zaid bin Hartha, as in-charge of the affairs at Medinah when he had to absent from the city to preside over any military expedition.[31] Meanwhile, prophet presided over four major expeditions, Badr, Uhad, Khandaq and Mecca respectively, as commander in chief of the Islamic forces against the Quresh of Mecca, among which the last expedition (8 A.H) extended the boundaries of the Prophetic Islamic state, initially, up to Mecca, and later on to the entire Arabian peninsula. After the victory over Mecca the prophet sent ambassadors to kings and rulers of different empires and countries of the world and some of them like Najashi, the king of Ethopia, Mazar bin S 'adi, the ruler of Bahrain, and Jaifar and 'Abd, the co-rulers of Oman, accredited the Islamic state and sent their ambassadors, in response, to the Islamic state.[32]

The people of Yathrib, some time before the Hijrah, resolved to crown Abdullah Bin Uba'e as their King; according to legends, even the crown was prepared for him, but the prophet's arrival automatically cancelled the crowning ceremony.[33] This fact made it clear that the people of Yathrib were aware of the political consequences of the Prophet's Hijarat to their city and rendering faith upon him. Moreover the appointment of in-charge by prophet in his absence at Medinah and agreements with the surrounding tribes, erection of watching towers around the Medinah, coining of official seal and appointment of officers to different clans[34] also

---

[31] Ibne Hashsham, *Seerat,* vol II, p 238, from Naeem Siddiqui, *Muhsine Insaniat,* p 407

[32] Naeem Siddiqui, *Muhsine Insaniat*, p 642.

[33] Ibne Hashsham,vol II, p 234, from A.A.Maudoodi, *Tafheemul Quran*, vol V, p 508

[34] Prophet , after the victory of Mecca, appointed *walees*, the governors to

determines that the prophet was also aware of his position as a head of state.

Writers in this topic, in general, were inclined not to use the term 'state' for the order established by the prophet in *Yat͟hrib*. *Ibene Tamaiya* named it as ' a kind of social order that clearly resembles a state[35] and E.I.J. Rosenthal as ' statute of *Medinah*.[36] Many ancient, medieval and modern writers have the same line of thought; but, a detailed analysis of the conditions of ' the order ' or the shows the presence of all the four, and even the fifth, essential elements of the state, i.e., population, territory, organisation and sovereignty, required by many of the modern political thinkers to recognise any congregation of the people as a ' state '. Hence, it was a ' state ' in modern political terms, as it was a state during caliphate or there after. Muhammad (s.a.s.) was, besides the prophet, in his *Madinatul Fad͟hilah*,[37] or *Nubuwwah*,[38] defender of the faith and the faithful, the dispenser of justice, the leader in prayer, commander in war, teacher and trainer in civilisation, all in one. It was, in weberian sense, a prismatic model.

But the form of the government prevailed during the

---

different areas and Ammal, the collectors of different taxes to different clans. Prophet retained Bazan bin Sasan, who was governor of Yemen from King Kisrah of Iran but later accepted Islam, as the governor of Yemen and after his death the province of Yemen was divided in number of small provinces and Shaher bin Bazan was appointed as wali of San'a, Zayad bin Lubaed of Hadhre Maut, Abu Moosa Ash'eri of 'Adan, Mu'az bin jabal of Jand, Abu Sufiyan bin Harab of Najran,Yazid bin Abu Sufiayan of Taymami, and 'Itab bin Aseed of Mecca.(Idrees Kandhalvi, Seertul Mustafa, p 72-73

[35] Prof. Qamaruddin : The politial thought of Ibene Taymiyah , page 52.

[36]7.E.I.J. Rosenthal, Political Thought in Medieval Islam, p 25

[37] The term for the Prophetic state coined by Al Farabi

[38] The term for the Prophetic state coined by Ibn Taymia

Prophet's period, that is termed as *Nubawwah* by Ibne Taimiyya,[39] was specific and a privilege only to the Prophet's, and not to be adopted as a general course in Islamic polity. The prophet exercised the power by virtue of his prophethood. He was neither elected nor chosen by the people but appointed by the God Almighty, the real sovereign; he was His messenger, vicegerent and representative; while as the general Islamic form of government prevailed during the orthodox caliphate was based upon rather the concept of vicegerency of Prophet, not of God, and these vicegerents were to be elected by the Muslims in general or selected by *As haabe hallo aqd*, the learned men among them. All the four orthodox caliphs were appointed by the later method.

----

[39] Prof Qamaruddin, *Political Theory of Ibne Taimiyya*, p

Ch : III.
Islamic State under Orthodox Caliphs

The Islamic state, during the period of the four orthodox caliphs, was almost a prototype of the Prophetic state, with the exception that the Head of the state was rather vicegerent of the Prophet and not of the God. The Caliph was, like the prophet, defender of the faith and the faithfuls, the dispenser of justice, the leader in prayer, commander in war, all in one. It was still a prismatic model.

Hzt. Abu Bakr, titled as *Khalifat-ur-Rasool,* was a businessman and even after assuming the responsibilities of the caliphate he thought of continuing his routine for getting the livelihood for kith and kin; but Omar, realising the need of a full-time caliph and complexity of the august office, refrained him from his previous routine and convinced the people to award salary to the caliph from *Ba'etul Mall*, the public exchequer.

Masjid-e-Nabawwi, the prophet's mosque was, besides the place of prayer, the headquarter, the parliament, the secretariat, the supreme court, the public exchequer, all in one, of the Islamic state. The caliph leads the prayer, address and consults the people, dispenses the justice, resolves the disputes, receives the ambassadors, appoints the governors and officials, formulates policies, plans for military actions, in this mosque. There were no standing armies; each and every Muslim citizen of the Islamic State was a soldier, off course voluntary and unpaid and defending the sate was their foremost obligation. The state was divided into *wilayahs*, the provinces, and the caliph was the authority to appoint the *Walees*, the governors to these provinces.

The four orthodox caliphs strictly have adhered to the Quranic injunctions and the prophetic guidance, drawn from the practices of the Prophet in the Prophetic state, in dealing with the governance of the Islamic State. Thus, following were the fundamental characteristic features of the orthodox Caliphate:

1. Elected Vicegerents:

All the four orthodox caliphs were elected by, offcourse not by the western standards, either by the Muslims in general or by the *As hab-e-Hall wa Aqd,* the learned men among the Muslims. Hzt. Omar proposed, immediately after the prophet's death, Hzt. Abu Bakr's name before the people as the successor of the prophet and the people of Medina, who were, in fact, enjoyed the status of the representatives of the Muslims, took the *ba'et*, the investiture, on his hand.[40] Hzt. Abu Bakr, eventhough, appointed by the Prophet as *Imame Namaz* in his death-bed, and given investiture by the senior

---

40 Narratd Anus bin Malik that ' Omar sat on the day following the death of the Prophet, recited the Tashahhud while Abu Bakr was silent, Omar delivered his speech that:

" I wish that Allah's Apostle had outlived all of us but if Muhammad is dead Allah, nevertheless, has kept the light amongst you from which you can receive the same guidance as Allah guided Muhammad with that. And Abu Bakr is the companion of Allah's Apostle; He is the second of the two in the cave; He is the most entitled person among the Muslims to manage your affairs. Therefore, getup and swear allegiance to him ".

Some people had already taken the oath of allegiance to him in the shed of Bani Sa'ad, but the oath by the public was taken at the pulpit. I heard Omar saying to Abu Bakr on that day "get on the pulpit" and kept on urging him till he ascended the pulpit where upon all the people swear allegiance to him.(Bukhari, Sahih, Eng. by Mohsin Khan, Vol IX, p 248.)

companions of the prophet in the shed of Bani Sa'idah, resorted to take the opinion of the common people in the form of ba'et, the investure, before assuming the charge of the caliphate. According to some traditions he refrained himself from taking major decision as long as the confirmation of *ba'et* is not received from the people of far-off places, such as Yemen, of the Islamic state.[41] The fact that none among these learned men raised the bogey of his kin-relation with the prophet manifests that there was no question of heredity in succession in Islam.

Hzt. Abu Bakr, nearing his end, appointed Hzt. Omar as his successor and justified it on the ground that he is the ablest person to shoulder this responsibility. Traditions report that he addressed a public gathering and taken the consent of the people before finalising the will of succession.[42]

Hzt. Omar, on the other hand, barred his son from succession and limited himself to propose six eminent, pious and rather popular persons before the people to choose any one among them. This Hexagon, in turn, delegated the responsibility of seeking and selecting the caliph according to the public opinion to Abdur Rahman bin Auf, one among the six but withdrawn voluntarily from the list. He after consulting the people from different walks of

---

[41] Al Kardari, vol II, pp15-16

[42] Hzt. Abu Bakr, before finalising the will of succession addressed the gathering in the Prophet's Mosque. He said:

"Do you agree on him whom I am appointing my successor. God knows, I have racked my brains as much as I could and I am not proposed any of my relatives to succeed but the Omar, son of Khattab. Hence, listen and obey him.

The people then responded: "we shall listen and obey to him". (At Tabri, *Tariq ul Umam w al Malook*, Urdu Trans. Ibrahim & Rashid Ahmed, Idara-e-Tableegh-e-Deen, Deoband, vol II, p 253)

life in Medinah as well as the passing pilgrims, caravans and tribes concluded and declared that the majority of the people are in favour of Osman; hence, the august office of caliphate was presented to Hzt. Osman.[43] In the modern terminology, Ibne Auf acted as election commissioner and followed, after short-listing the candidates to two, Ali and Osman, the sample-survey method, andafter analyzing the public opinion declared Hzt. Osman as the popular most, hence, elected candidate.

Hzt. Osman could not find the opportunity to take any action, as he was assassinated, in this regard and Hzt. Ali refused to appoint the successor; hence, Hzt. Hassan was elected as caliph by the consent of the majority of the people.[44] The last instance shows that the kin-relation with deceased or out-going caliph was not a disqualification, as it was not an essential or desirable qualification, to succeed a caliph.

It is evident from these facts that all the four caliphs assumed the august office by the popular consent and concurrence those who appointed by the out-going caliph also resorted to take the *ex post facto* investiture. All they agree, in principle and practice, that it's the peoples or their learned men's, not one or the few person's, prerogative to elect the caliph. Hzt. Omar, during the last year of his reign, came to learn some one's design to install his choice as caliph by taking *ba'et* on his hand. He expected that such investiture would establish that person as caliph as Omar's investiture had established the caliphate of Abu Bakr well

---

[43] At Tabri, vol III, p 296, Ibne Atheer, vol III p 34-45, Idaratu Taba'tul Muneriah, Egypt, 1356H; Ibne s'ad, Tabqat, vol III, p 344; Dare Sdir, Beirut, 1957; Fathal bari vol VII, p 49

[44] Ibne Katheer, Al Bidaya wan Nahaya, vol VIII, pp 13-14, Maktabatu S'ada, Egypt; Al Mas'oodi, vol II, p 42.

enough.[45] Hzt. Omar reacted sharply and resolved to address the people and clarified his stand in Abu Bakr's instance and questioned that 'Ye! Who amongst you is there a match with Abu Bakr in stature and popularity? He warned stern action against making this exception as precedent and sanctioned capital punishment for both, the initiator of *ba'et* and for whom the ba'et is conducted.[46] According to another tradition, He ordered that 'Kill him ye who seeks caliphate without consultation and by coercion'.[47]

Traditions report that on the eve of Hzt. Osman's assassination some well wishers of Ali approached him and persuaded him to assume the caliphate but he refused and declared

---

[45] The reference was to the abrupt arising of Omar from his place during the meeting at Shed of Banu Sa'idah when he proposed Abu Bakr's name as the caliph and extending his hand to him offered ba'et, the investiture. There was no lengthy deliberation before electing Abu Bakr.

[46] Hzt. Omar, who proposed Hzt. Abu Bakr, heard some one, during his last Hajj, saying that 'I'll ba'et on so and so's hand and his caliphate will be established as Omar's ba'et had established Abu Bakr's caliphate'. He reacted sharply to this and soon after his return to Medina he addressed the people and clarified his stand on ba'et on Abu Bakr's hand that how in exceptional circumstances he had suddenly risen to propose Abu Bakr and offered investiture to him. If that was successful, he continued, let it not be made a precedent. He, further, questioned that 'Ye! Who is as distinguished and popular amongst you as Abu Bakr? He warned, whoever will swear allegiance to another without consultation with other Muslims, he and the one whose allegiance is sworn shall both stand to die. (Bukhari,Sahih, Kitabul Muharibeen, Ch XVI; Ahmed, Musnad, vol I, Hadith No 391; Ibne Hajar, Fathul Bari, vol, II p 125.)

[47] At Tabri, vol 3, p 292; Ibnul Atheer, vol III p 34-35, Muneer, Egypt; Ibne Sa'ad, Tabqaat, vol III, p 344, Dare Sadir, Beiroot; Fathul Bari, vol VII, p 49

in unequivocal words that ‘it's the prerogative of *Ahl-e Shoorah* and *Ahl Badr* to decide the matter of succession to caliphate; and he who will be chosen by them will be the next caliph; we will meet and decide the matter.[48] Tabri quoted the words: ‘My Ba'et can not be held secretly; it must be only with the consultation of the Muslims.’[49] Then in a public gathering at *Masjide Nabawwi* almost all the Muhajireen and Ansar taken ba'et on his hand. Only 17 or 20 distinguished companions abstain themselves from the *ba'et*.[50] On his deathbed some persons inquire with Hzt. Ali that shall we *ba'et* in favour of Hasan; He replied that 'I will neither order, nor forbid you from such act; you can see for your self. Some well wishers, when he was expressing his will at deathbed, suggested him to appoint his son as his successor but he refused and replied that’ I’ll leave the Muslims in the condition in which the prophet left them.[51]

These historical facts made it clear that there was an established consensus among the early caliphs and the companions of the prophet that the caliphate is an elective post that is to be filled with the mutual consultation and the consent of the Muslims and their independent will; and the Authority established on the principle of heredity or by coercion was *Mulookiat*, Monarchy, that is far from being Islamic, not the *Khilafat*, the Islamic vicegerency. Another significant event that proves the democratic and elective nature of the caliphate beyond any iota of doubt is Hzt. Hussain's stand on Hzt. Mu’awiay’s will of succession and Yazid’s authority. He refused to *ba'et* in favour of Yazid, declared his succession as ultra virus to the *shari'a* and resistance of such unlawful authority

---

[48] Ibne Qutaibah, Al Imamah was Siayasiah, vol I, p 41.

[49] At Tabri, vol IV, p 112

[50] At Tabri, vol III, p 450-452

[51] Ibne Katheer, Albidaya wan Nihaya, vol VIII, p 14, Maktabae Sa'ada, Egypt; Al Mas'oodi, vol II, p 42

as a religious obligation. He resisted it practically by whatever means at his disposal. Those who abstained themselves from this endeavour were also agreed with him in principle but they were well aware of the cowardice and fragile nature of the people of Kufa, hence, the consequences of the endeavour.

2 - Government by Consultation:

All the four caliphs adhere strictly to the principle of consultation. They were not to take any major or policy decision without consultation among the senior and distinguished companions of the prophet. Traditions report that Hzt. Abu Bakr, when confronted with any issue, used to refer Quran at first instance, and if he could not find the matter in that then approach the *Sunnate Nabi*, still unresolved he consult the pious and learned among the companions and act according to their suggestion. Hzt.' Omar also followed the same path.

Each and every participant of the *Majlise Shoora*, the consultative council, off course informal, enjoys maximum liberty and freedom to express their views and criticise the caliph or his policy. Hzt. Omar announced the official policy of the caliphate in this regard in his inaugural speech to such a consultative council that:

> "I have called you here for nothing but that you may share with me the burden of the trust that has been reposed in me of managing your affairs. I am but one of you, and today you are the people that bear witness to truth. Whoever wishes to differ with me is free to do so, and whoever wishes to agree is free to that. I will not compel you to follow my desires."[52]

---

[52] Abu Yousuf, Kitabul Khiraj, p 25

3 - Public Exchequer - a Trust :

The orthodox caliphs always regarded *Bait ul Maal*, the exchequer as a trust from God and the people to them, not as their own treasury. They did not consider it permissible to receive into it or expend from it a sum, which the law did not authorise. Utilising it for personal purpose was simply unlawful to them. Hzt. Omar in a speech remarked: "Nothing is lawful for me in this trust of God save a pair of clothes for the summer and a pair of clothes for the winter, and subsistence enough for an average man of the Quraish for my family. And I am just one of the Muslims."[53] In another speech he compared the responsibility of holding the exchequer to the responsibility of an orphan's guardian with the orphan's property, that if he is needy he can take the needful, otherwise he shall not take any thing.[54]

Ali, at war with Mu'awiyah, was exhorted by some of his well wishers to use the exchequer to win adherents against him who was drawing large numbers to his side by giving sumptuous rewards and gifts. But Ali declined that counsel saying "do you want me to win success by unfair means?[55] His brother Aqil wished to be

---

[53] Ibne Katheer, *Al Bidaya wan Nahaya*, Matba't al Sa'adah, Egypt, vol VII, p 134

[54]Hzt. Omar in a speech represents the orthodox caliphs' attitude towards the exchequer:

"I do not regard anything appropriate in respect of this trust of yours but three things: that it should be taken by right, that it should be expended by right, and that it should be withheld from wrong. My position regarding this property of yours is the same as that of an orphan's guardian with the orphan's property. So long I am not needy I will take nothing from it. When I am needy I shall take as it befits one to take from an orphan's property under his care." (Abu Yousuf, *Kitabul Khiraj*, p 117)

[55] Ibn abi Al Hadid, *Sharh Nahjul Balagha*, Dar al Kutub Al Arbiyyah,

helped by the exchequer, but he refused by saying, "do you wish your brother to give you the money of the people and take his way to hell?[56]

4 – The Aim & Objective of the Govt.:

The aims and objectives, ideal and purpose of the government under orthodox caliphs can be traced from their speeches and sermons delivered at different occasions from the Caliph's pulpit. Hzt. Abu Bakr, in his first sermon in Masjide Nabawwi, after assuming the charge of the august office said:

> "I have been made a ruler over you though I am not the best of you. Help me if I go right; correct me if I go wrong. Truth is faithfulness and falsehood is treachery. The weak one among you will be strong with me till I have got him his due, if God so wills; and the strong one among you will be weak with me till I have made him pay what he owes, if God so wills. Beware when a nation gives up its endeavours in the way of God, He makes no exception but brings it low, and when it allows evil to prevail in it, undoubtedly He makes it miserable. Obey me as long as I obey God and the Prophet; if I do not obey them, you owe me no obedience."[57]

And Hzt. Omar in a speech expressed the position of the caliph in these words:

> "No ruler holds so high a position as to have the rig to command obedience in defiance of God. O people, you have rights on me whom I shall relate before you, and you may take me to task over them. I owe you this that I

Egypt, 1911, vol I, p 182

[56] b. Qutaibah, *Al Imamah was Siyasiyah*, Matba'at al Futuh, Egypt. p.71.

[57] At Tabri, vol II, p 450; Ibne Hashsham, al sirat ul Nabawiyyah, Matba'ah Mustafa al Bai, Egypt, 1936, vol IV, p 273

do not receive anything from your revenues of the fai' (lands or possessions that accrue to Muslims in consequence of their collective dominance, not as booty in war) given to us by God except in accordance with the Law, and that nothing that accrues to us in these ways should go from the treasury but rightfully."[58]

Omar instructed his governors, before sending them off to their provinces, in this wise:

> "I have appointed you governor over the followers of Muhammad, peace be upon him, not to make you masters of their persons and properties but to enable you to lead them to establish prayer, dispose of their affairs with justice, and dispense them their rights among them with equity." [59]

Once he declared in public that " I have not sent my governors that they may whip you and snatch your property, but that they may instruct you in you faith and the way of your prophet. If there be any who has been treated otherwise, let him bring to my notice. By God I will that his wrong be avenged. Upon this 'Amr bin 'Aas, governor of Egypt, stood up and asked, "what, when a man is appointed ruler and he chastises someone, will you take revenge on him?" Omar replied in unequivocal words, "Yes! By God, I will take revenge on him. I have seen the Prophet of God himself allowing people to take revenge on him." [60]

5 - Rule of Law:

Rule of law prevailed under the orthodox caliphs. They did

---

[58] Abu Yousuf, *Kitabul Khiraj*, p 117

[59] Al Tabri, vol II, p 273

[60] Abu Yousuf, *Kitabul Khiraj*, p 115; Abu Dawood al Taylisi, *Musnad*, Tadition No 55; Ibne Al Athir, vol III, p 30; *Al Tabri*, vol III, p 273)

not regard even themselves above the law. On the other hand they declared that they stood at par with any other citizen, Muslim or non-Muslim, in this respect. Judges had to be appointed by them; but once a person was appointed he was free to deliver judgement against them as against anybody else. Once Caliph Omar and Ubayy bin Ka'eb differed in a matter, and the dispute was referred to Zaid bin Thabit for decision. He disturbed to some extent due to presence of caliph before him as a party in dispute and tried to pay due regard to the him; but, Hzt. Omar preferred to be treated at par with the opposite party and remarked that Zaed is unfit to be a judge as long as Omar and an ordinary man did not stand equal in his eyes.[61]

This equity and equality was not limited to the Muslims. During Ali's reign he himself saw a Christian selling his lost coat of mail in the market of Kufah. He did not seize it from the fellow with a ruler's might, but preferred to brought the case before the magistrate concerned; and as he could not produce adequate evidence to support his claim, the decision of the court went against him.[62] Ali, when appeared as a party, during his own Caliphate, in Judge Shuraih's court he rose to greet the Caliph. Ali remarked " this is your first injustice''[63] While the head himself came under the

---

[61] Once Caliph 'Omar and Ubayy bin Ka'eb differed in a matter, and the dispute was referred to Zaed bin Thabit for decision. The parties appeared before Zaed, he rose and offered his own seat to 'Omar, but 'Omar sat by Ubayy. Then Ubayy preferred his claim which ' Omar denied. According to the procedure, Zaed have asked 'Omar to swear an oath but Zaed hesitated in asking for it. 'Omar himself swore an oath, and at the conclusion of the session remarked that Zaed was unfit to be a judge as long as 'Omar and an ordinary man did not stand equal in his eyes. (Baehiqui, Al Sunan ul Kubra, Daerutul Mu'arif, Hyd, 1936, vol I,p 136.)

[62] Baehiqui, *Al Sunan ul Kubra*, daerutul Muarif, Hyd, 1936, vol I, p 136.

[63] *Walayat ul A'yan, Maktabatul Nahzatul Misriyyah*, Cairo, vol II,p 168.)

preview of the law the question of others will not arise. Omar collected all his governors at the annual pilgrimage and announced in a general congregation of people that if there was a person who had a charge of injustice against anyone of them, he should come forward to make his complaint. One person rose from the multitude and complained that he had been undeservedly given a hundred stripes by Amr bin Aas. Hzt. Omar asked him to come forward and square the account with him. Amr bin Aas protested, beseeching Omar no to expose his governors to this humiliation, but, Omar reiterated that he had seen the Prophet of God himself allowing men to avenge themselves upon him, and asked the aggrieved man to step forward and take his revenge.

6 - Absence of Bias:

Another distinctive feature of the orthodox caliphate was that everybody received an equal and fair treatment exactly in accordance with the principles and the spirit of Islam, the society of those days being free from all kinds of tribal, racial or parochial prejudices. As the Prophet of God passed away, the tribal jealousies of the Arabs rose again like a heldup storm. Tribal prejudice formed the main impulse behind the claims to prophethood and large-scale apostasy that immediately followed the Prophet's demise. But when the people realised that Abu Bakr and in his wake Omar, dispensed exemplary, even-handed justice not only among the various Arab tribes but even among the non-Arabs and non-Muslims, and that they did not show any favour or even preference to their own nearest kith and kin, the old biases were instantly repressed and Muslims were once more inspired with that cosmopolitan outlook which Islam sought to inculcate in them. Abu Bakr and Omar's attitude in this respect was most exemplary, while Hzt.Osman could not maintain that standard. After death of Hzt. Osman, Ali tried to recapture the standard set by Abu Bakr and

Omar. He had no bias in him and proved himself remarkably free from it. Abu Sufayan had tried to excite this passion in him on Abu Bakr's accession. He had asked him "How could a man of the humblest family in Quraish become Caliph? If you prepare to rise, I will undertake to fill this valley with horsemen and soldiers." But Ali had coldly retorted that this spoke for his enmity to Islam and the Muslims. And so far as he was concerned, he regarded Abu Bakr truly fit for that august office."[64] Hence, when he rose to the caliphate he treated the Arabs and non-Arabs, gentlemen and poor born Hashmites and others, all alike. No distinction was made between them, even between Muslims and non-Muslims in the matter of justice; none received preference over the others undeservedly.[65]

7 – Democratic Spirit:

Another significant feature of the Islamic Vicegerency was its democratic spirit. There was liberty of expression, save heresy, and criticism, in maximum, against the Caliph, without any kind of fear of persecution. All the four orthodox Caliphs were, as they live like a commom man, participate, five times a day, in congregational prayers, and walk on the roads, always in access to every one. There was neither palace, nor any security personnel to the caliph. Affairs of the government were transparent to public. Meetings of the consultative council used to hold openly and the participants express their views without any fear or hesitation. Caliphs not only allow but, rather, encourage criticism against them.[66] There was no ruling and opposition party but each and

---

[64] At Tabri, vol II, p 449

[65] Ibn abi al Hadid, *Sharhe Nahjul Balagha*, vol I, pp 180-182

[66] Hzt. Abu Bakr, in his first sermon after assuming the august office said: "I have been made a ruler over you though I am not the best of you.

every member of the community used to put a vigilant eye upon the conduct of the government. Prophet's instruction that "witnessing truth before a despotic ruler is also a *jihad*" charged them to point out the tiniest flaw of the Caliph. Once, for instance, Hzt. Omar was at the stake for his, as assumed by the critic, excess in distribution of the cloth.[67] In another occasion he had to withdraw his decree, regarding the *Meher*, when an old woman criticised his stand on the ground of a Quranic injunction.[68]

Hzt. Osman, during his reign faced severe criticism, frequently, but did not resort to calm down or prosecute any critic. He tried his best to elucidate the facts before the public. Hzt. Ali also tolerated the blasphemy of the Khwarjites against him. Once one Kharji who was announcing publicly 'By God! I will kill Ali,' were brought before him, but Hzt. Ali released them and said his well wishers that I can not sanction any punishment to them only because they are expressing intention to kill me, until they

---

Help me if I go right; correct me if I go wrong. Truth is faithfulness and falsehood is treachery. (Tafseer Ibne Ka<u>th</u>eer, with reference to Hzt.Abu Bakr Y'ala and Mun<u>dh</u>ar, vol I, p 467)

[67] During the reign of Hzt. Omar, Hzt. Salman Farsi, rose to question, when Hzt. Omar was delivering Friday prayer from the pulpit of Masjide Nabawwi, that how he acquired two pieces of the cloth while all the others received only one. Hzt. Omar, instead of giving answer directly, turned his face towards his son, Abdullah bin Omar, and he clarified that he has surrendered his share in favour of his father, to enable him to make a garment.

[68] Hzt. Omar in one of his sermon expressed his intention to limit the amount of *meher* to four hundred Dirhams, but an old woman pointed out his flaw, at the by quoting an Ayah of Quran which allow a lot of goods as meher. Then Hzt. Omar reiterated from his intention. (Tafseere Ibne Ka<u>th</u>eer, with reference to Abu Bakr Yala and b. Mun<u>dh</u>ar, vol I, p 467.)

practically try some thing to do so.[69]

----

[69] Most of the above references have been taken, as it is without *Cf*, from Maududi, A.A. *Khilafat wa Mulookiat,* and *Islami Riyasat*.

Ch. IV.
Transformation into Monarchy

It was the misfortune of the humankind, particularly of the Muslims, that the noblest form of Government, namely Islamic Vicegerency could not last long for more than three decades and transformed into the traditional monarchy.

The deviation from the main course, and transformation of Vicegerency into monarchy, began with the appointment of Yazid, the son of Hzt. Mu'awiayh, as the successor to the august office and taking ba'et, the investiture, by coercive means made it a permanent phenomenon of the Muslim polity. By this act Hzt. Mu'awiayh completed the transformation of Khilafat, the Vicegerency, into Mulokiat, the monarchy. Hzt. Mu'awiayh was also well aware of the theoretical implications and practical consequences of his innovative acts. Traditions report that once he admitted 'I am the first monarch amongst the Muslims'.[70] On another occasion he warned the people 'I was not unaware while taking the reigns of power in my hands that all of you were not happy with me; I know what is in your hearts but I acquired this power by sword. Hence, if you have observed that I am not giving your rights properly, be patient with the little.'[71] In brief, this deviation ruined the noble and democratic characteristics of the Islamic Vicegerency and cultivated the following characteristics of the traditional monarchy that were quit contrast to the spirit of Islamic Vicegerency:

---

[70] Al Iste'ab, vol. I, p 254; *Al Bidaya wan Nah*aya, vol. VIII, p 135

[71] Ibne Katheer, *Al Bidaya wan Nahaya*, vol.VIII, p 132

Change in appointment-procedure of the Caliph

Hzt. Mu'awiyah's usurpation of the caliphate by coercive means and, further, appointment of his son as the successor to caliphate was a major deviation from the usual and legitimate procedure of the appointment of the caliph. This act transformed the caliphate from an elected office to the hereditary one. Hzt. Hussein sacrificed his life to stop this transformation and to set it on the right tracks but in vain.

All the four elected caliphs have neither aspired nor sought the office but Hzt. Mu'awiayh employed all the means at his disposal, without bothering their legitimacy, to seek the caliphate for himself and to retain it in his family, Banu Umaiyyah, forever. He rebelled against the elected caliphs, Hzt. Ali, and Hzt. Hassan, one after another and compelled the later, by deploying his loyal armed forces in and around the capital, to surrender the caliphate in his favour. After assuming the office he adopted all coercive means to take *ba'et*, the investiture, in his favour. It was quite contrast to the precedents and like putting the cart before the horse; the usual procedure, during the reign of the orthodox caliphs, was to take the charge of the office after the establishment of the *ba'et* and not to seek the *ba'et* with the influence of the office. Similarly, he did not spare any stone unturned to impose his son upon the people. He offered gifts,[72] threatened, forced, and deceived[73] the people to

---

[72] Hzt. Mu'awiayh send one lakh Dirham to Hzt. Abdullah b. Omar to obtain his ba'et but he refused the offer(Ibnul Atheer, vol. III, P 25; Albidaya wan Nahaya, vole VIII, p 89)

[73] When 'Abdullah b. Zubaer and some other senior companions refused to ba'et in favour of Yazid, Hzt. Mu'awiayh warned them 'By God! If any one of you uttered a single word against me the sword will be faster on his head than his next word. Furthermore, he called his bodyguard and instructed him to cut their heads immediately if any one of them try to

accept his son, Yazid, as the next caliph. From the day of Hzt. Mu'awiyah's usurpation of the office to the dissolution of the caliphate by Mustafa Kamal Ataturk it was in vogue to install himself as caliph by virtue of heredity or power and then to compel the people to obtain *ba'et* in his favour. Those who refused had to face dire consequences. *Ba'et* was no longer an instrument of election of the caliph; but, rather, it became a formality to impose a religious obligation up on the people to obey the *de-facto* ruler, without bothering how he acquired the office.

Change in life style of the caliph:

The orthodox caliphs led a life of comman, rather poor, man of the Islamic state. The salary fixed for Hzt. Abu Bakr was only four thousands Dirham per annum. They were always in access to the comman man; they walk in the streets, purchase for the household needs in the market-yard; lead the prayers five times a day in the mosque; patrols during nights to help the needful. There was neither any palace, nor the security guards to them. A stranger, during the reign of Hzt. Omar, wandered the streets of the Medinah for hours and hours to find out, at last, that there is no palace for his caliph. But this new breed of caliphs, more precisely Kings, at once adopted the life style of the traditional Monarchs of the Iranian and Roman empires. They started to live in palaces; employed numerous bodyguards; separated themselves from the common people. They were out of access to the Common man. Gradually

---

open their mouth and in that condition brought them before the people of Mecca and stated before them that 'these are the noblest and wisest people amongst you to be consulted before deciding any important issue; they have agreed to ba'et in favour of Yazid. Therefore, you should follow them. Then people of Mecca resolved to ba'et; otherwise they are not to do so.(Ibn Atheer, vol. III, p 252)

they alienated from the daily prayers and during the Friday prayers also they segregated themselves from the common people either by barracks or a huge number of bodyguards.

Exchequer converted into Royal Treasury

The orthodox caliphs regarded the public exchequer as a trust of the people in their hands. Hzt. Omar explicitly compared it as a trust of an orphan in his trustees hands that if he is in need, he is authorise to take the needful and otherwise he should not take any thing from it. Hzt.Abu Bakr had drawn eight thousand Dirham, four thousands per annum, from the exchequer during his reign as salary but returned the entire amount through his will, at the time of his death.[74] Hzt. Omar declared that his salary will be equal to the earning of an average person of Qureish and nothing else.[75] Hzt.Ali also maintained the same standards while Hzt. Osman was wealthy, hence, did not draw any thing for himself. Hzt. Ali refused to grant any thing from the exchequer to his own brother Aqil[76] and rejected the suggestion to grant the people from the exchequer, when he was at war with Hzt. Mu'awiayah, to win adherents for his caliphate.[77]

In contrast to these luminous precedents the Umayyads and the Abbasids caliphs transformed the exchequer into the Royal treasury. They had the opinion that they are accountable to none for the appropriation from the exchequer. Deviation in this regard began with Hzt. Mu'awiayah himself. He opened the exchequer of the Syria that was under his governorship, to draw large numbers to his side and against the caliphate of Hzt. Ali. After assuming the

---

[74] *Kanzul Aamal,* vol. V, p 2280

[75] Ibne Katheer, *Al Bidaya Wan Nahaya*, vol. VII, p 134

[76] Ibne Alhadid, *Sharhe Nahjul Balgha*, vol. I, p 182, Darul Kutubul Arbia, Eqypt,1329

[77] Ibne Qutaiba, *Al Imamah was Siayasah*, vol. I, p 71.

charge he continued the rewards and grants in order to obtain *ba'et* for him and his son.[78] Moreover, they, instead of a fixed salary taken the entire *Bait ul Mal* in their disposal and drawn the entire expenditure of their pomp on it liberally, without bothering its legitimacy. They followed the Persian and Roman Emperors in their life style. When Hzt. Omar b. Abdul Aziz, the fifth and the only right-going caliph from the 'Umayyads, assessed the illegitimate property of the Royal household he found property worth forty thousand Dirhams per annum with himself.[79]

In levying the taxes also they ignored the precedents as well the obvious injunctions of the Shari'a. Hzt. Omar b. Abdul Aziz in his reign listed out several taxes that were in force against the Shari'a.[80] The explicit instance in this regard was the continuation of levying *Jizya* upon the neo-Muslims.[81]

Lack of the Freedom of Expression

The orthodox caliphs allowed freedom of expression and criticism, in maximum, against their personal and public decisions. They had several luminous instances of tolerance of severe criticism, even the threat to kill, in their account. They never prosecuted, rather encouraged, any one for expressing his opinion against them.

In quite contrast to these liberal precedents the Umayyed and Abbasid rulers at once censored the freedom of expression.

---

[78] Hzt.*Mu'awiayah* sent One lakh Dirham to Abdullah b. Omar to obtain his ba'et but he refused to take(Ibne Atheer. vol. III, p 25; Ibne Katheer, *Al Biday wan Nahahya*, vol. VIII, p 89);

[79] Ibne Atheer, vol.IV, p 164; Ibne Katheer, Al Bidaya wan Nahaya, vol. IX, p 163

[80] At Tabri, vol. V. P 321; Ibne Atheer, vol. IV, p 163.

[81] Ibne Atheer, vol.IV, p 79

Any one who dared to criticise them had to lose his life. Hzt. Mu'awiayah started this tradition with the assassination of Hzt. Hajar bin Adi, the senior companion of the prophet, with seven other companions, on the charge of criticising the Umayyed governor of Kufa for his cursing upon Ali.[82] Marwan, governor of Medinah, from Hzt.Mu'awiayah, asked the people to ba'et in favour of Yazid but when Abdur Rahman bin Abu Bakr refused to do so he ordered his arrest.[83]Abdul Malik Bin Marwan during his visit to Medinah warned the people that if any one uttered 'fear the God' I would kill him.[84] Waleed bin Abdul Malik ordered to kill the person who reminded him of *'Asr*, evening prayer.[85]

Such despotic acts of these so-called caliphs buried the freedom of expression so deeply that it could not born again among the Muslims.

Dependent Judiciary

Judiciary under the orthodox caliphs was independent from the executive. Although the caliph appoints the judges but he was not authorised to interfere in their affairs and to be dealt at par with comman man when he had to appear before the court. Hzt. Omar appeared personally in the court of Zaed when he and Uba'e b. Ka'ab developed differences in a matter. At the conclusion of the session Hzt. Omar remarked, for Za'ed's undue respect towards him, that Za'ed is ineligible to hold the post as long as the caliph and a comman man did not stand appear equal in his eyes.[86]

---

[82] At Tabri, vol. IV. pp 190-207; Ibne Atheer, vol. III, p 234

[83] *Al Isteab,* vol. II, p393; *Al Bidaya*, vol. VIII, p89; *Ibne Atheer*, vol. III, p 250.

[84] Ibne Atheer, vol. IV, 401.

[85] Ibne Abur Rabi, *Al Aqdul Fareed*, vol I, p 62, Cairo, 1940

[86] Baihaqi, *Al Sunan ul Kubra,* Daeratul Muarif, Hyd, 1936, vol. I. p 136.

Similarly, Hzt. Ali approached the court when he saw his lost coat of mail with a Zimmi, but he lost his case as he could not present sufficient evidencc before the court.[87]

As against to the above instances Umayyed and Abbasid caliphs turned the judges into mere puppets and the courts as instruments of their despotism. No Judge could dare to accept a case against even the courtesans or the officers of the Empire, no need to mention their position against the caliph. Even the governors of the provinces were authorised to dismiss the judges.[88] Under these caliphs the judicial offices lost their significance and dignity to the extent that pious and God fearing jurists, such as Imam Abu Hanifa and Imam Malik, preferred prosecution and punishment to these offices and whoever accepted them lost his reliability among the people. There were very few among the Judges, like Imam Abu Yousuf, who could sustain their independence and, hence, credence.

End of Consultation:

Consultation with the people was the basis of the orthodox caliphate. These caliphs conduct consultative meetings with the people of knowledge and piety and decide the matters according to their suggestions. These people regard the suggestion as a trust and provide it independently without any fear. They were free to criticise the policy and person of the caliph and the caliphs encourage and acknowledge such criticism. It was not only a consultative body of secular legislation but also the apex institution of interpretation of the Holy Text and the path of Prophet and

---

[87] Walaytul A'yan, Maktabatul Nahdat al Musriyya, Cairo, 1948,Vol. II, p 168.

[88] Sueti, Hasan ul Muhasirah, *Al Matbatush Sharfia*, Eqypt, Vol. II, p 88.

deducement of religious regulations. Decisions given by this council enjoys the status of the consensus of the Ummah.

But with the transformation of Caliphate into Monarchy this principle also changed and the people of knowledge and piety were replaced by the courtesans. These people could not dare to criticise or even to give any suggestion against the Royal preference. They always after the wish and will of the caliph and support it without bothering its appropriateness

Hence, the apex consultative council loses its popular as well as religious status. The pious and reliable persons alienated with it. Its decisions no longer enjoy the status of consensus of Ummah. People started to look after the private institutions of different jurists, such as Imam Abu Hanifa, Imam Malik. This strange situation created chaos in jurisprudence. The Judges began to follow different jurists according to their personal choice and some time differences aroused between the judges and the jurists. Consequently, a wide gulf developed between the secular and religious realms.

End of the Rule of Law

Rule of law is the basis of the Islamic State and Shari'a law of the land. No one can seek exemption from the law, nor even the caliph. The orthodox caliphs adhered to this principle strictly. They never sought any exemption from the law or privilege for themselves or their relatives and applied the law without any bias. The Prophet himself declared that even if his daughter committed theft she would also punished. He permitted his companions to take the retaliation if any excess had done to them unintentionally. Hzt. Omar stoned, according to some traditions, his own son to death for committing adultery.

But, the 'Ummayed and Abbasid at once rejected this

principle. They declared themselves, in unequivocal words, as above the law, they never hesitated to breach the laws publicly. Hzt. Mu'awiayah sanctioned capital punishment for several persons, including some senior companions of the Prophet such as Hajr b. Adi, Ummaar b. Yasir, without any legal ground. His successor Yazid assassinated the very kith and kin of the Prophet in Karbala and mutilated their death bodies. He instructed his governor Muslim bin Uqba to capture the Medina, the city of Prophet, and to permit his soldiers, after the victory, for three days to do as they wish. His soldiers massacred the men and children and raped the women and girls during these three days. Traditions report that at least eleven thousand people killed and the actual number of rape-victims can be estimated by the fact that one thousand women became pregnant by the rapes.[89] After finishing with Medina the same force turned towards Mecca and stoned the *Ka'aba*.[90]

They transgressed the Shari'a in general principles also. For instance, during the reign of Prophet and the orthodox caliphs Muslims were not to receive inheritance from their non-Muslim relatives and vice versa, but Hzt. Mu'awiayah violated the Shari'a and provided the Muslim with the right of inheritance into non-Muslim relatives'property.[91] Amount of retaliation, according to Sunnah, is equal for the Muslim and the Zimmi, but Hzt. Mu'awiayah changed it and made it half for the Zimmi.[92] Inclusion

---

[89] At Tabri, Tareekhul Umam wal Mulook, Vol. IV, pp 372-379 & Ibn Katheer, Al Bidaya wan Nahaya, Vol. Pp 219-221.

[90] At Tabri, Tareekhul Umam wal Mulook, Vol.IV, p 383; Ibn Katheer, Al Bidaya wan Nahaya, Vol. VIII, p 225; Ibn al Atheer, Al Kamil fit Tarikh, Vol. III, p 316.

[91] Ibn Katheer, Al Bidaya wan Nahaya, Vol. XI, p 232

[92] Ibid, Vol. VIII, p 139

of Za'ed bin Sumayya, who was illicit son of his father, into his family is another transgression of Hzt. Mu'awiayah.[93] He made even the Muslim women captured in internal wars as slaves.[94] He declared all his governors and officials, apart from his family, above the law and immune from the retaliation.[95] These are the few among the numerous instances of the transgressions made by none other than Hzt. Mu'awiayah. No need to mention the excesses and oppressions of his successors and the tyranny of the Abbasid.

Racial and Tribal prejudices:

Another distinctive feature of the reign of the orthodox caliphs was the absence of racial and tribal bias. Each and every, during these days, one received fair and equal treatment in accordance with the principles and spirit of Islam. With the establishment of Umayyed Monarchy, that was based upon the parochial prejudice, the tribal jealousies and the nationalistic feelings of the Arabs and Non-Arabs rose again like a held up storm. Tribal and parochial prejudices formed the main impulse behind the claims of the caliphate by Hzt. Mu'awiayah and later by Abbasid and Alvis respectively. During these regimes parochial and racial prejudices and discrimination on the basis of birth and race became the order of the day. Umayyed monarchy was predominantly and explicitly an Arabian regime. It was, from the beginning, based upon the assumption of superiority of Arabian race. The concept of equality among the Arabs and Ajamees, non-Arabs was, for them, a relic of past. There was discrimination in each and every sphere of life. Ajamis were ineligible to be appointed as governors, judges and

---

[93] Ibn Al Atheer, *Al Kamil fit Tarikh*,Vol. III, p 220.

[94] *Al Iste'ab*, Vol. I, p 65.

[95] Ibn Katheer, *Al Biday wan Nahaya*, Vol. VIII, p 71 & Ibn al Atheer, Vol. III, p 248.

even as leader in prayer.[96] They expelled from the cities like Basra.[97] *Jizya* continued upon them even after conversion to Islam. State attitude towards the Ajamees changed the public opinion as well. There was a wide spread discontent among the Arabs when none other than Sayeed bin Jubaer appointed as the Judge of Kufah; hence, the judicial office transferred to Abu Burdah, who was poor in jurisprudence but an Arab.[98] Marriage of Arabian girl with Ajami boy was to be regarded as null and void, for all practical purposes.[99] This humiliating attitude of the authorities, on the one hand, and the general Arabian people, on the other, encouraged Shu'obiat, Ajami Nationalism among the non-Arab population of the Islamic empire.

Umayyed's Policy of discrimination was not limited to the Ajamis. Infact, it rejuvenated the tribal prejudices among the Arabians. Government itself exploits these traditional rivalries to further its own aims. The Governors shower rewards upon their own tribe and oppresses the rival one explicitly. Abu Muslim Khurasani exploited the rivalry between Yamani and Mu<u>dh</u>ari, two dominant tribes, to overthrow the Umayyed regime and to establish the Abbasid.[100]

---

[96] Ibn Abde Rabbi, *Al Aqd ul Fareed*, Vol. II, p 233.
[97] Ibid, Vol. III, p 416.
[98] Abu Burdah instructed to decide the matters with the help of Saeed. (Ibn Khullakan, Vol. II, p 115)
[99] Abul Faraj Isfahani reports that the Umayyed governor of Medina dissolved the marriage of an Arabian girl with a neo-Muslim Ajami, punished the bride-groom with twenty lashes and humiliated him to the possible extent.(Al Aghani, Matbatul Misriyah, Egypt,Vol. XIV, p 150)
[100] Ibn Asakar reports that the rivalry between these two tribes reached to the extent, when the Abbasid forces were advancing towards Damascus, that two Members and Mehrabs were eructed in mosques, one for the Yamani and another for the Mudhri. (Ibn Katheer, *Al Bidaya wan*

Religion-Politics Dichotomy

The orthodox caliphs were not only the temporal rulers of the state but the spiritual leaders and guides of the *Ummat-e Muslima* as well; hence, they called as *Ameer ul Mumineen*. They led the daily and Friday prayers, *Hajj*, and other congregational religious obligations. Their consultative council was, apart from parliament, the apex religious authority to interpret and deduce the laws from the Quran and the Sunnah. It was the symbol of the consensus of the Ummah in religious matters. All the Muslims regard its decisions as religious obligations and follow them by depth of their hearts, since the caliph as well as the members of the consultative council used to be the most pious, God-fearing and the most knowledgeable figures among the Muslims.

However, the transformation changed the entire scenario. The august office lost its respect, reliability, and significance as Yazid assumed the caliphate. He was the least reliable and pious among the Muslims and his companions, who form consultative council of the Islamic State, were like him. He and his companions transgressed almost all the limits of the Shari'a. They lack religious knowledge and piety and greedy of power and authority. His successors, except Omar b. Abdul Aziz, follow suit. Hence, the caliphate and his consultative council lost its spiritual significance and religious authenticity among the eyes of the Muslims. These caliphs were not ignorant of the reality; hence, they alienated themselves with the religious ceremonies and began to appoint any pious, knowledgeable and reliable persons as in-charge of religious affairs. People also began to look after the private councils of jurisprudence established by pious, reliable and knowledgeable persons, such as Imam Abu Hanifa, Imam Malik etc. Thus, began

---

Nahaya, Vol. X, p 45.)

the religion–politics dichotomy that culminated in the division of secular and spiritual authority between *Sultan and Khalifa* by Fatimids.[101]

----

[101] Most of the above references has been taken, as it is without *Cf*, from Maududi, A.A. *Khilafat wa Mulookiat,* and *Islami Riyasat*.

Ch: V.
Muslim Political Thought: Early and Medieval Periods

Infact, each and every aspect of Islam, including political, has its roots in the Prophetic era. However, this era was free from theo-political controversies as the very source of Sharia was alive. The reign of the first two Caliphs also had no major upheaval, with an exception of one brief controversy over the succession of the Caliphate after the Prophet, at the theoretical side.[102]

However, from the third caliph onwards controversial political discourses, primarily due to expansion of the boundaries and inclusion of alien nationalities into the fold of Islam, have been emerged that, being combined with the *realpolitik* issues, culminated into the civil war among the Muslims themselves. These wars, in turn, generated numerous new theological debates among Muslims with regard to the following issues:

- Who was right / wrong in these battles and why?
- If both were right / wrong what is the ground for holding such an opinion?
- What should be the attitude of the Muslim community towards a usurper or tyrant?

These debates naturally led to the induction of certain opinions

[102]This controversy was on the issue that who will succeed after the Prophet, a *Muhajir* or an *Ansar*? However, it was settled peacefully within hours with intercession of Hzt. Omar and, consequently, Hzt. Abu Bakr was chosen as Caliph, almost, unanimously.

and justifications for such opinions. This phenomenon gradually developed distinct sects among Muslims such as Shiite, Khwarjite, Mu'tazilite, Murjite, etc, having their own set of theo-political principles and ideas. These sects fashioned as religious but in reality their base was merely political.

After the demise of the fourth Caliph Hzt. Ali the Islamic vicegerency, that was more or less democratic, transformed into a hereditary monarchy. Imam Hussein strived hard at the practical front to restore the pure but in vain.

Henceforth, intellectual emphasis had shifted from political to spiritual, on one hand and rather the quest for truth to mere justification of prevailing regime on theological grounds, on the other. The pure and honest element of intelligentsia felt alienated and resorted to the spiritual while the opportunist employed all their potentials to cook justifications for unjustified acts of the established regime. Hence, politics became the haven of the opportunists. Consequently, religion-politics dichotomy became apparent among Muslims. Certain sincere theologians could dare even their life to challenge the authority with regard to certain theological principles without bothering of its political bearings, but, with the bitter experience of the earlier reformist movements, they preferred stability to the legitimacy of prevailing regime and pronounced resistance even against a usurper or tyrant ruler as illegitimate and sin. Such candid pronouncements of honest and otherwise daredevil-theologians provided a theological ground to opportunist Muslim thinkers to deduce justification for their Master's deeds.

The cause and formation of major sects and their political ideology, as well as the views of eminent Muslim thinkers, sincere as well as opportunists, on political issues is being elucidated here.

Shiite:

The first and foremost among the Muslim sects was the *Shi'an-e-Ali,* the party of Ali, abbreviated in course of time as *Shi'a*. Though, few companions of the Prophet belonged to Hashemite descendant regarded Ali, on account of his close relationship with the Prophet, as the preferable and more entitled successor for the Caliphate, but until the reign of Osman these opinions had not assumed a sectarian-form. However, during the reign of Ali they emerged as a distinct sect with a set of views on Caliphate, that was termed by them as Imamate.

Their theory revolved round Ali. Caliphate for Hzt. Ali, and for his descendants there after, was their primary concern. They hold the opinion that Ali was *Afdhal,* the preferable, among all the companions of the Prophet; hence, the Caliphate was due to him as an undeniable privilege but confiscated by the impostors, namely Abu Bakr, Omar and Osman. Therefore, they were not the legitimate Caliphs and their Caliphate was null and void. Moreover, Ali was the first legitimate *Imam*[103] and after him it was the exclusive privilege of his descendants. Some of the Shiite limited the Imamate further to the Fatimide lineage of Ali.[104]

Moreover, for Shiite, Imamate is not a public office to be elected by the people but a pillar and foundation stone of faith. It is a primary obligation of the Prophet, and thereafter of the Imam, to nominate the successor. Hence, the Prophet nominated Ali as his successor. For them, Imam is impeccable and free from all sins and immune to error.

The concept of Imamate generated another theological discourse that what is the legal position of the Imamate of the

---

[103]Shiite term for the Caliph.

[104]Ibn Khalladun, *Muqaddamah*, p. 196.

preferred in presence of the preferable. Sunnites, and Zaedites among the Shiites regarded it perfectly legitimate while the other Shiite sects assumed it as illegitimate. The above concept and creed caused several uprisings by the late successors of Ali and ultimately resulted in downfall of Umayyads.

The fundamental distinction between the Shiite concept of Imamate and Sunnite concept of Caliphate was that the former regarded it as a religious obligation while as the later taken it as a secular / temporal necessity.

Khwarijite:

The second sect emerged among the early Muslims was the Khwarjites, who suddenly abandoned Ali, while he accepted the arbitration of the Abu Moosa Ashari and Umroo b. Aas, on the assumption that he committed a sin by accepting the arbitration of man instead of God. For them, Sin was synonymous with infidelity. Hence, they declared Ali and the majority of the Muslims as infidels.

They acknowledged Abu Bakr and Omar as righteous caliphs but could not extend their tolerance towards Osman. In their opinion, Hzt. Osman, in his later period of reign, erred from the path of justice, hence, deserved to be deposed and killed. Ali also, according to them, was not a righteous Caliph and deserved to be killed due to acceptance of Human arbitration. Ali, Muawia and all those who agreed to the arbitration were sinners, hence, infidels. All the Khwarjites, except Ibbadhiyyah sect among them, considered war on and assassination of all other Muslims as a religious obligation. They acknowledged *Qur'an* but rejected Hadith and *Ijma'*.

In fact, the Khwarjite views were quite opposite to the Shiite. According to them Caliphate is a public office, hence, the Caliph

must be elected by the free will and vote of the Muslims. They regarded, in quite contrast to the Shiite, Quraishite descent as unessential to hold the Caliphate; they rather preferred a non-Quraishite, since, it would be easy to depose him if he turned despotic. The Caliph should be obeyed as long as he acted righteously and justly; but if he forsakes the right path he must be deposed of or assassinated. A large group of Khwarjites, called as Najadiyyah, did not see any need of the state at all; they believe that the Muslims should abide the right by themselves.[105]

Mu'tazilite:

Mu'tazilah, the Seceders, was another sect that originated during this tumultuous period. According to the popular opinion of this sect, appointment of Imam was a religious urgency and he must be elected by the consensus or at least by the majority of the Muslims. Some of them insisted on consensus and advocated suspension of the election if the community could not reach to the consensus. The community should choose only morally qualified and efficient person as Caliph; Quraishite descent is irrelevant. Some of them preferred a non-Arab or freed Slave, since it would be easy to depose him if he turned tyrant. Indeed, they were more concerned with removal of the Caliph than stability, hence, preferred a weak government. Some of them regarded the Imamate or the State as a superfluous office and unnecessary institution.[106]

---

[105]Abdul Qahir Baghdadi, *Al Farq Bain al Firaq*, pp. 55-99, 315, cited in Abu Zuhra Misri, Urdu tr. Ghulam Ahmed Hariri, *Hyat-e-Abu Hanifa*, Aijaz Publishing House, New Delhi, 1998, pp. 215-237.

[106]Al Masudi, *Muruj al Zahab*, p.191, cited in Maududi, *Khilafat-wa-Mulukiat*, p. 202.

Murjite:

Extremism of Shiites, on one hand, and the Khwarjites on the other, originated a passive middle course called Murjiah. They were neutrals in the civil war between Ali and Muawiah as they could not decide who was on the right path and who on the wrong. Hence, they were not to blaspheme any of the belligerents and left it to God to decide the affairs between them. The most important of their beliefs was that Actions' do not affect one's 'faith'; hence, any sin can not turn a Muslim into infidel. However, the most important belief, that had a political bearing, was that if upholding right and forbidding wrong involves use of arms it must be avoided. It was right to check misdeeds of others, but to resist a tyrant Muslim Imam was not allowed since it will weaken the power of Muslim nation.

In fact, these views strengthened the position of impostors and discouraged resistance-movements among the Muslims.

Sunnite:

These circumstances, however, could affect only a minority of the Muslims. *Suad-e-A'zam*, the majority, being still adhere to the Sunnah, given birth to some of the eminent scholars and jurists who defined the creed and tenets of the Muslims, on the light of the Qur'an and authentic traditions of the Prophet, in an unequivocal and convincing manner.

There was a consensus among the Sunnite regarding the position of the orthodox caliphs that all the four were righteous and preferable in the order of their succession and that Muawia was the first Monarch among the Muslims. They regarded all the companions of the Prophet with due respect and mentioned all of them in good manner. They had the opinion that the God Almighty only will resolve their internal disputes and others need not discuss them.

They regarded the Caliphate as rather more secular and less religious necessity. For them, it was not one of the fundamentals of faith and religious practice but one of the *furu'*, details, connected with the acts of the believers; and the appointment of Imam is enjoined on *Ummah* by *al-sam,* tradition, that comprises *Quran, Sunnah* and *Ijma'*.[107] Hence, the congregational religious obligations such as daily and Friday prayers, *Hajj, Nikah, Talaq* will be continued lawfully even in absence of the caliph.[108]

Caliphate of *Mafdhool,* the preferred one, in presence of *Afdhal,* the preferable, is perfectly legitimate. Sunnites have taken guidance from the historical precedents of the orthodox caliphs in determining the legitimate method of appointment of the Caliph. Both, 'the election by at least one qualified elector' and designation of 'one or more immediate successors from other than the close relatives' by out-going Caliph, are the equally legitimate methods of succession to Caliphate.

The Caliph must be a Quraishite free-born male Muslim. However, a considerable number of Sunnite jurists preferred stability and peace to the legitimacy of the incumbent in Caliphate. According to them if any Muslim usurped the Caliphate by whatever means, and established *sharia* and peace, then he became, for all practical purposes, like a legitimate caliph and it is obligatory upon the people to render obedience to him and to follow him in congregational religious rites; it is forbidden to rebel

---

[107] *Ummah*, Muslim community; *Quran*, the Holy Book revealed by the God Alimighty on Prophet Muhammahd, *Sunnah*, the path of Prophet Muhammad, *Ijma'*, the consensus of those who know among the Muslims.

[108] *Hajj*, the annual congregational-worship at Mecca, *Nikah,* the marriage, *Talaq*, the Divorce.

against or resist him.[109]

However, Abu Hanifa, the most followed jurist among the Sunnite, and his contemporary, Malik b. Anas, had divergent opinion regarding the Caliphate of impostor.

Imam Abu Hanifa:

According to Abu Hanifa (80/699-150/767) all the four caliphs were righteous and preferable in the order of their succession. All the companions of the Prophet were also righteous and respectable. He did not hesitate to mention that between Ali and Muawia, the former stood by right more than the latter, yet he refrained from inflicting reproach on the other.

In his opinion, faith was synonymous with owning and believing and action was different from the faith and vice versa. Hence, sinners among the followers of the Muhammad were all believers, not infidels.

Abu Hanifa differentiates between a legitimate Caliph and an impostor. According to him, the caliph should be chosen after consultation with *As Hab-ur-Rae,* i.e. those who are entitled to give opinion. Seizing power by force and later seeking allegiance by coercive mehods is not an appropriate and legitimate method. However, all the functions, secular as well as religious, of the society may be carried on lawfully under such imposter. If a judge himself is just his decisions will be lawful, even though he was appointed by an imposter; Hajj and prayer may be lawfully offered behind such imposters despite their illegitimacy.

Nevertheless, he neither equates the impostor with the duly

---

[109]Abu Zuhra, tr. Raees Jafri, *Hyat-e-Ahmad*, Aijaz Pub, Delhi, 1998, p. 264.

elected caliph nor regards the resistance against such imposers as unlawful. On the contrary, he practically pronounced his opinion on the issue by favouring the resistance of Nafs Zakiyya. He asserted that the Caliphate of an unjust incumbent was basically wrong and insupportable, and deserved to be overthrown.[110] In his opinion, people not only have the right, but it is their duty to rise in rebellion against the usurper; that such rebellion is not only allowed but obligatory provided, however, that it promises success in replacing the tyrant or transgressor by a just and virtuous ruler, and not to end in mere loss of lives and power.

Abu Hanifa was particularly conscious with regard to the freedom of expression. According to him, Qur'ãn itself provides this freedom as a right as well as duty by its ordain *Amar bil Ma'roof wa Nahi Anil Munkar*', i.e. enjoining the right and forbidding the wrong. He asserted the right of freedom of expression even against law-courts. He never hesitated to point out the flaws in judicial decisions of his times. Respect of the court, for him, did not mean letting the courts to deliver wrong decisions. He did not consider it lawful to imprison a person who spoke ill even of a legitimate caliph, not even if he went to the extent of abusing the caliph and expressing intention to kill him, until there was a resolve on his part of an armed revolt or breach of peace. He expressed these views under the tyranny of Umayyads and Abbasids and paid the cost of his life. He, by the order of Mansoor Abbasi, sent to jail and later killed by instilling poison in his food.[111]

---

[110]" My covenants does not extend to the wrong doers".(Al Quran, 2:124)

[111]Shibli Nu'mani, *Seerat-un-Nu'man,* p 45.

Imam Malik b. Anas:

Malik b. Anas (93/712-183/801) also expressed similar views with regard to the revolt against the impostor. Though, he avoided direct criticism against Abbasids regime but when Nafs Zakiyyah revolted against it he supported his claim and endeavour for the Caliphate by issuing a *Fatwa*, religious ordain, that pronouncement of *Talaq*, divorce under compulsion, hence *bai't* (investiture) by coercion, is null and void. Abbasids prosecuted, humiliated, and punished Malik but he did not eat back his ordain.[112]

It was Nafs Zakiyyah's claim for the Caliphate on which the two divergent sects, Shiite and Sunnite (at least Hanifites and Malikites among Sunnite) agreed, practically though not theoretically.

In fact, Abbasids deceived Alvis in their struggle for Caliphate. When Abu Hisham Abdullah Alvi, the fourth Imam of the Alvis, reached to his end in Syria he could not find any Alvi at his disposal. Hence, appointed an Abbasid, Muhammad Abbasi, as his successor.[113] When Hashemite succeeded in their struggle against Umayyads, Abbasids drawn advantage from this nomination and installed themselves in Caliphate and started persecution of Alvis, like their predecessors. They pressurised sincere and famous theologians to provide theological justification to their regime.

Qadhi Abu Yusuf:

Abu Yusuf (113/731-182/800), the most capable disciple of Abu Hanifa, presented his political views in his treaty *Kitab-ul-Kharaj,* written in his capacity as the chief justice and law minister of the Abbasid kingdom as a hand book for the Caliph to deal with

---

[112]S. Suleiman Nadvi, *Hayat-e-Malik*, Dairatul Mu'arif, Lucknow, p. 57.
[113]*Ibid,* p. 55.

the affairs of the state. His views are in fact the soft version, softened to suit with the arbitrary nature of the Abbasids regime particularly of the Caliph Harûn Al Rashid, of his master Abu Hanifa's views. He did not compromise with his creed but presented it in a convincing fashion.

His main concern in his treaty was to initiate the Abbasid Caliph to relinquish the Iranian and Byzantine traditions and revert to the traditions of righteous Caliphs without invoking the royal wrath.

He tactfully avoided the discussions regarding the appropriate procedure of election of the Caliph, legal position of the impostor, *Shura* etc., but did not hesitate to mention that the Caliph would be responsible not only to God but also to the people. He insisted upon the people's right to criticise their rulers and that such criticism contributes to the good of the people and the State.

He mentioned, first time in the history of Muslim political thought, the duties of the Caliph in an organised manner. The Caliph, according to him, must establish the rights of God and enforce the limits prescribed by Him; determine, and ensure the availability of, the rights of other right-holders; to revive the conventions of the virtuous rulers; check the injustice and redress the grievances of people after proper scrutiny; command the people to obey the God and stay away from sins; apply the Law of God on himself and others alike, without regard to who suffers by it and make only lawful exactions from people and spent them in lawful means. He disallowed the practice to acquire one's land forcibly and bestows it to other. He insisted upon the personal liberty. Nobody, according to him, can be imprisoned on mere accusation without a regular trial. He vehemently advocated for independence of judiciary and condemned the court-official's interference in course of justice.

Similarly, he enumerated the duties of the citizens as well.

They have to obey their rulers, should not commit acts of disobedience, not should lift arms against them, not reproach them unnecessarily, or deceive them. They have to share their excesses, to help others, and to co-operate in lawful matters.

He wrote unequivocally that the exchequer was a trust of God and the people, not the personal property of the Caliph. The Caliph is asked to forbid his officials to spend public money for their private needs. He authorised the caliph to impose taxes in addition to those imposed by the *sharia.* However, the taxes should be levied by the consent of the people and only the surplus wealth should be taxed. Further, no one should be taxed more than his capacity and the amount should vary according to the capacity of the tax payer. It should be collected from the wealthy and spent on poor. Tax-rate should not be fixed rigidly, nor should be extracted by coercive means.

He, like his master Abu Hanifa, presented strikingly liberal principles regarding the non-Muslim subjects of an Islamic State. According to him, the Islamic State should observe the agreement faithfully, whatever it may be, made with *Dhimmis*, they will be free from the responsibility of the defence of the state, and they should not be burdened with excessive poll tax and land revenues. Moreover, he recommended exemption from poll tax to the poor, the blind, the old, recluse, workers at the places of worship, women, and children.

In fact, his intention in the treatise was not to present the ideal Islamic political theory but rather to present a constitutional frame work that, in addition to satisfying the minimum conditions required for an Islamic State, would be practicable in the peculiar circumstances of the Abbasids regime.[114] Thus, it was the

---

[114]Qadhi Abu Yousuf, *Kitab-ul-Kharāj*, cited in Maududi, *op cit*, pp.. 76

beginning of a new era in the Islamic political theory in which the stress was shifted from the ideal Islamic form of the Government to the best possible, practicable and presently acceptable one.

Imam Ahmad b. Hanbal:

Imam Ahmad b. Hanbal (164/788-241/853), in contrast to the Imam Abu Hanifa and Imam Malik, had given preference to the stability than legitimacy. According to him, it was obligatory to obey the Imam of times, no matter he took the office by force of sword or by the consent of the people. He disallowed resistance against the established authority, even if it was established by illegitimate means. In his opinion, it is unlawful to curse on such imposter caliph or to dispute with him. It is obligatory to follow him or his appointees in the Friday prayer and those who repeat such prayers were innovators and opponents of the Sunnah. And whoever rebelled against a Caliph, whose caliphate has been accepted by the people either by consent and initiation or by coercion and compulsion, has broken the power of believers and went against the way of the Prophet; and if he died in such a state of rebellion it would be a death of pre-Islamic days of ignorance.[115]

Shafi'i also had similar views with regard to the rebellion against impostor.

.

.

.

Medieval Period

Advent of the Islam and the Islamic State in the far away lands

---

262-274.

[115]Abu Zuhra, *op cit*, p. 264

of Asia and Europe and translation of the intellectual material of these countries into Arabic brought some new and strange elements, such as logic, philosophy, metaphysics, into the realms of the Muslim knowledge. These new elements, especially the Greek and Roman philosophy, influenced the Muslim intellectuals, in general. An attempt is being made to present the political ideology of such eminent philosophers and thinkers of the early and medieval Islam.

Al Farabi:

Al Farabi (258/870-339/950), preoccupied with the Greek philosophy on one hand and the Islamic ideals on the other, tried his best to synthesise Plato-Aristotelian philosophy and Islamic tenets. He, following Plato, began his theory with the analysis of human nature. According to him people differ in their physical strength and intellectual capacity; hence, the Imam must be the most capable in all the virtues of humankind; he must be self reliat in all fields and possesses excellence in sciences and arts.

Al Farabi, under the profound influence of Plato, had a concept of *Madinat-ul-Fadhilah*, namely Ideal State. It is the excellent and perfect state while as there may be imperfect states also viz. *Madinat-ul-Fasiqah, Madinat-ul-Jahilah* and *Madinat-ul-Dhallah*, i.e. the evil doing state, the state of ignorance and astray-going state, respectively in their imperfection. These remind the Aristotle's classification of states.

Madinat-ul-Fadhilah will be the state administered by the best and most talented one; he must aim at the prosperity and happiness for all the residents of the state. The Imam, chief of this state will preside in all fields of life. He must be excellent and perfect in his profession to achieve the highest happiness in the stae. He will not be subservient to any one. He must be in possession of the following twelve characteristics:

1. Sound health and perfect organs.
2. Intelligence and sagacity.
3. Good memory.
4. Prudence and talent.
5. Eloquence.
6. Devotion to education and learning.
7. No greed for food, drink, play, and sex.
8. Friendliness towards truth and truthful persons.
9. Vastness of heart, loving nobility, and natural magnanimity without meanness.
10. Indifference to wealth.
11. Devotion by nature to justice and just people.
12. Strong resolution, courage, and promptitude without any sign of fear.

If the people could not find any one of these qualities, the laws promulgated by the former chief should be kept in force. The second chief who succeeds the first should fulfil at least the following six qualities. He must be:

1. Wise and philosophical;
2. Learned man;
3. Expert in deduction of laws when not available in *Shari'a*;
4. Farsightedness;
5. Well experienced and eloquent in enforcement of *Shari'a*;
6. Physically suitable for, and skilled in, warfare.

The sovereign will be called as *Imam-us-Sunnah*, the chief of tradition, and the state as *Muluk-us-Sunnah*, the country of tradition. The sovereigns of the ideal state who succeed one after another will be all like one soul as if there were one king who continued all the time. The people of the ideal state must have something common in their learning and acting though different groups of people may have some sciences and deeds peculiar to them. They achieve happiness through both of these qualities.

The rulers of imperfect states, in quite contrast to the above, lack the above qualities of the ideal state. Both, the rulers and the ruled, in the evil-doing states are like weeds in a field. They would be like savages and could have no organisation worthy of a State.[116]

Although, the ideal state of al Farabi is derived from Plato but the main difference between the two is that the Platonic State was limited to a city while the Farabi's *Madinat-ul-Fadhila* may be international and global-state in character.

Al Mawardi:

The main concern of Al Mawardi (364/974-450/1058) was to assert the authority of Abbasid caliph against the Buwaihid Amirs and provide theological justification to their regime. His treatise, *Al Ahkam-us-Sultaniya,* was intended to demarcate the spheres of authority between the caliph (the religious head) and the Amir (head of secular administration) on the basis of a negotiated agreement. However, he disallowed, in contrast to al Baghdadi, simultaneous existence of two caliphs.

Mawardi insists that the necessity of Imamate arises on the basis of the Ordains of the Allah given in Qur'an, chapter IV, verse

---

[116]Saghar Hasan Al Ma'sumi, "Al Farabi", in M. M. Sharif. ed. *History of Muslim Philosophy,* in 2 vols, Otto Harrasowitz, Weisbaden, 1963, vol. I., pp. 707-717.

64.[117] According to him Imamate is established to replace prophecy in the defence of the faith and the administration of the world and it is demanded by *shar'* itself. This statement is directed against the Mu'tazilete as well as philosophers like al Farabi, who derived the state from the reason. He has drawn a distinction between 'government based on reason' and 'government based on revealed law'. He gives prefrece to he latter and regard it as the higher form. In his view the earlier provides protection merely against mutual injustice and anarchy while as the second provides positive enforcement of law and justice in mutual confidence and friendship in this world and prepares the man for the world hereafter.

Al Mawardi, like al Baghdadi, insists on the election of the Caliph by the *Aš haab ul Hall wal Aqd*, the qualified electors, but he accepted the nomination of a successor by the ruling Imam, for instance, of a son by his father. The electors must possess *Adala*, justice. According to him, the Imamate can be established by a contract between two parties namely, *Imam* and the *jama'*, i.e. the ruler and the ruled ones. *Ijma'*, the consensus, is required to conclude the contract and it can be concluded only after the *bai't*, the investiture, by the qualified electors.

If a contract is concluded and a caliph assumed the office he can not be replaced even by a man more worthy than him, unless he forfeits the Imamate by loss of freedom. The loss of freedom can happen in either of two ways, viz. he may be captivated, thus become unable to exercise his functions, and second, an Amir may seize his effictive power and may place him under restraints. In the

---

[117]"We sent; no messenger save that he should be obeyed by Allah's leave. And if, when they had wronged themselves, they had but come unto thee and asked forgiveness of Allah and asked forgiveness of the messenger, they would have found Allah Forgiving, Merciful"(4:64)

latter case the preferable candidate must appear on the scene after the investiture and the contract between *Imam* and *Jama'* (the Leader and the People) have taken place again.

Al Mawardi regarded the nomination by the out going Caliph as an equally legitimate method. He justified it on the historical precedents of Abu Bakr's nomination of Omar and Osman's succession to Omar. He regarded appointment of 'six candidates to chose from them' by Omar as nomination, while as all other jurists regarded it as election. By these two precedents he tried to legitimise the hereditary transfer of power within the Abbasids dynasty, whose interests he intended to promote. He, to further their interests, insisted that it is a religious obligation upon the out-going caliph to nominate his successor. He, to justify the above method, introduced a new element namely *Masalih Amma*, i.e. the public welfare, into the theory of Caliphate. He, on the basis of nomination of three successive generals by the Prophet during a war deduced the provision to designate three successive heirs. In order to legitimise Al Mansur's act of replacement of his predecessor's successive nominees by his own appointees Mawardi has provided the first successor with the power to cancel his predecessor's nominees after assuming office.

The principle of election is affirmed only when the out-going caliph appointed two successors without assigning priority to any one of them and this can be happened only after the death of the present caliph.Mawardi assigned ten principal duties to Caliph, viz.

1. Protection of the faith;
2. Provision of justice;
3. Protection of the territory of the Islamic State;
4. Enforcements of punishments as ordained by God Almighty;
5. Waging Jihad against those who invited to Islam but

refused to accept it or to pay *jizya*;

6. Just distribution of booty;
7. Charity;
8. Maintenance of state-finance in appropriate manner;
9. Selection and appointment of competent officials;
10. Personal supervision to the public affairs.

Finally, Mawardi discusses the conditions for the effective maintenance of the Imamate and the valid grounds for its forfeiture. In his view, Imam forfeits his authority if he lost physical or mental fitness. Here, he stressed upon the Caliph's ability to interpret the faith correctly and to maintain his freedom. Again, contemporary situation is responsible for this detailed and precise exposition.[118]

Nizam ul Mulk Tusi:

Niżam-ul-Mulk Ṯusi (408/1018-485/1092) was the product of a tumulus period that witnessed the decadence of the Caliphate to its lowest profile. In his times it degraded to puppetry in the hands of powerful emirs. He, fortunately, got appointment as *Vizier*, the prime minister by a Seljuk Amir, Alp Arsalaṉ. Hence, he devoted his attention to provide a theoretical basis and working model to this office that lacks prcedence. He selected novel institutions and non-traditional subject matters, *Sultan* and *Vizier,* for his political treatise, *Wasaya*, and developed the theories of *Sultanate* and *Vizierate*, i.e. the kingdom and the ministry respectively.

Though, he was not the first one to discuss the above institutions but certainly he was the first to apply a realistic approach, while the previous writers stuck to the legal one. He realised that it was the independent rule of *Sultan,* i.e. the de facto emir, and not that of the Abbasids Caliph, under whose rule the

---

[118] E. I. J. Rosenthal, *Political Thought in Medieval Islam*, pp. 27-37.

people had actually been living; and that the Caliph by legitimising the authority of *Sultan* only recognised his *de facto* sovereignty *ipso facto,* hence, this practice did not render him subordinate to the Caliph. His political theory represents a particular phase of development of the Muslim polity in which the powerful emirs seized the authority of Caliph and made the latter a puppet.

Tusi, in his political discussions, consciously avoided any reference to the Caliph as the *de jure* head of the Muslim community and always mentioned his master as *Padshah*; thereby he escaped discussing legal relations of the Caliph and the Sultan. He, at the instance of the Seljuk ruler Malik Shah, compiled *Siyasat Namah.* His main concern was to assert his master's claim to sovereignty and to counter the Mawardi's *Ahkam-us-Sultaniyah* that had been written at the instance of the Abbasids Caliph to vindicate his claim to sovereignty. This indicates a theoretical conflict between the powers of the Caliph and the Sultan.

Tusi presented the theory of Divine Right of Kings to assert the independent position of his master. The Caliph, under this theory, was no longer the real source of authority as it was transferred to the Divine directly, in first place and next to the ability of the imposter. He, in his *Siyasat Namah*, presents:

> "In every age God selects one from the mankind and adorns him with princely skills, and entrusts him with the affairs of the world and the comfort of the subjects".[119]

He, further, justified not only the usurpation of the authority but the despotism and bloodshed of the kings over the subjects, as he regarded it as the punishment of their misdeeds. He says:

> "Due to their sin they bring this wrath upon themselves. Benevolent kings disappear from amongst

---

[119]M. Ruknuddin Hasan, "Nizam al Mulk Tusi", in M. M. Sharif, vol. I., p. 756.

> them. Swords are drawn and bloodshed follows; and whosoever is powerful does as he pleases, till the sinners are perished in those calamities and bloodshed.--- Ultimately, power goes to one of the people whom God by His grace blesses with success according to his worth, and endows with wisdom and knowledge".[120]

He was equally emphatic on the principle of the hereditary kingship. The kingly office, for him, is essentially of Divine Origin as well as hereditary and should pass from father to son. Thus, he justified the claims of the Seljuk Sultans for the sovereignty on a three-fold basis, namely, the divine sanction, the conquest by power, and the hereditary succession.

He dealt with the question of obedience to the royal authority with the same point of view, namely divine origin of kingship. According to him, it is obligatory to worship the Almighty, and to obey the king since He appointed him. He consciously avoided the question of obedience to an unjust king, as his aim was to provide legitimacy to the absolute monarchy without any human restrictions. He never bothered to provide a rational or theological justification to any of his argument. For him, Monarch was the sovereign authority in his realm and source of all political power; all are subordinates to him and he is accountable to none, save God.

He, after providing the justification for his master's office, turned towards his own, *vizierate.* He was primarily, rather exclusively concerned with the political and moral aspect of this office. *Vizirate* to him was the most important and the most exalted office, next only to the sultanate. According to him 'it is the institution on which the religion and the kingdom, the state and the people depend'. He regarded it as an indispensable part in the machinery of a monarchical government. He argued:

---

[120]*Ibid,* vol. I, p. 756.

> "All the Kings who have left their good names in the pages of time, owe it to the felicity of the righteous vizier.---A good vizier brings to the king a good name and leads him to adopt a good conduct. All the princes who had been great, and whose name shall be held in honour till the Day of Judgment, were those who had good ministers".[121]

Throughout his argument he attempted to show that the vizier was actually responsible to Sultan for the entire administration, that is to say he is a share holder in the Sultan's real power. He not only exalted the office but also enumerated the dangers in having it. According to him there are at least five dangers, viz. injustice due to overburdening of work; pleasure of one and displeasure of many; incurring the displeasure of the royal house hold, and consequently of the king; hostility of nobles, grandees and courtiers; dependence upon the large number of officials whose conspiracy and lethargy undermine his reputation. He advised the vizier to overcome these dangers by showing due regards for the companions, courtiers, other favourites of the king and the nobles and high officials of the kingdom. The duties of vizier, according to him, are determined by the four-fold relations: First, he is under the obligation of obedience to God; secondly, he owes allegiance to his royal master; thirdly, he has to care for the favourites of the king; and fourthly, he is concerned with the common people.

In brief, Tusi, attempted to present the *vizierate* as a responsible and delicate office, requiring a man of sharp intellect and outstanding abilities.

Al Ghazali :

Al Ghazali's (450/1058-505/1111) theory of Imamate

---

[121] *Ibid,* vol. I. p. 770.

manifests the gulf between the theory of ideal caliphate based on the *Shara'* and the political realities of the Abbasid caliphate dominated by the Seljuk Sultans. It also represents the transformation from idealism to realism. It must be understood against the background of contemporary political and religious controversies and struggles.

In his early treaty, *Kitab-ul Iqteṣad fil I'tiqad*, he insisted Imama in its ideal form while as *Kitab-ul-Mustazhiri* is tempered with political realism and readiness to make concessions to the ground realities. Later, in his *Ihya-ul-'Uloom* he, in his attempt to preserve the caliphate as the symbol of unity, surrendered to the actual power of the Seljuq-sultans.

Al Ghazali, like al Mawardi, insisted that Imama is based upon Shariah, not reason; hence, he opposed philosophers' attemt to examine it by the yard-stick of Greek philosophy. He his view it is an indispensable institution of the Muslim life directed by the Ijma'. Moreover, it is necessary too as it is advantageous and keeps the damage away in the world. In fact, the good order of the religion is depend upon the good order of the world, which is possible only in presence of an Imam who is obeyed by the people. He used the word Sultan to denote the *Imama.* He quoted the *Hadith* that 'religion and politics are twins' and *din,* religion is foundation and sultan, power is the guardian. Here, in his theory, he stressed on power. He writes that it is significant though mere a mean to a very important end namely, good order of religion with *sadat-ul-akhira,* i.e. ultimate happiness.

He, like al Mawardi, enumerated the virtues of Imam by which he distinguishes himself among the other philosophers. However, he modified these virtues to suit the contemporary political situation and to the then-ruler, al Mustazhiri. For instance, prowess and courage has always been considered as necessary virtues of the Caliph, but Ghazali explained its absence pointing to the *shawka*, the power of Seljuk sultans, which guarantees prowess to the Caliph. Similarly he disposed off the awkward condition of *kifaya,* the competence to discharge the duties of governance, by stating that this condition is fulfilled as long as the Caliph is supported by competent *veziers*. He also treated the *'ilm* in the similar fashion. He introduced *wara'*, fear of God, piety and refraining from dubious practices, public concern and importance to the religion and politics, to compensate the lack of these virtues.

He provided legitimacy to the institution of Sultan by introducing the concept of delegation of the authority from the Caliph to the possessor of *shawkah*, the real temporal power. However, the ultimate responsibility lies with the Caliph. Ghazali, ultimately made the Caliph as one to whom the wielder of force gives his allegiance and confined the Caliph to the religious duties.

Further, he astonishingly accredited an existing practice of designating the Caliph by the Sultan, the *de facto* ruler.[122]

Ibn Jama'a:

Ibn Jama'a(639/1241-733/1333) further developed the Al Ghazali's views and taken them much nearer to realism. He justified the Imama on the authority of Qur'an, chapter 36, verse 26 and chapter 22, verse 41. He regarded it a religious necessity and God's Grace. He styled the ruler as *Zil ul Allahi fil Ardh*, i.e. the shadow of God on earth. He ordained, following the opinion of his Imam, Shafi'i that forty years of tyranny of an unjust ruler is better than the abandonment of his subjects for one hour.

He, listing the methods of installing a Caliph, includes nomination by the outgoing Caliph as an appropriate method. He, like al Ghazali, described three methods of installation of caliph viz. election, designation / nomination, and forceful seizure, but in

---

[122]E. I. J. Rosenthal, *Op. Cit*, pp. 38-43.

the third category he had gone beyond al Ghazali's designation of a Caliph by *de facto* ruler and includes usurpation of the Caliphate by a powerful military leader in the list. In other words, investiture-by compulsion (*bai't-e-Ikrah*) after seizing the power, designation, and usurpation, all three methods are equally appropriate to establish the authority of Caliph and there is no need of a contract. The people are bound to obey the Caliph by ordains of the Qur'an:

> "Obey Allah, his messenger and those who are in authority".[123]

He has taken the above verse to mean that God coupled the duty of obedience to those who are in authority with that to Him and his Prophet. He added *'ulama* also in this list under the guise of 'those who are in authority'. Hence, *bai't* under coercion is lawful and required obedience. He actually ruled that any usurper can acquire legitimacy and become a *de jure* Imam by a forceful *bai't*. By letting the king-maker make himself as king he come to an end of the way on which al Ghazali was already far advanced. Further, following the line of Tusi, he legitimised the delegation of the authority to the sultans or viziers by declaring it as a necessity and 'custom of our times'. Ibn Jama'a, like Al Mawardi, distinguished between *tafweedh* and *tanfidh* namely, vizirate of delegation and execution. The former implies independent conduct of all affairs of state guided by his own *ra'y* and *ijtihad.* Hence, he must have the same qualification as the Caliph himself, except Quraishite descent. He provided the Caliph with the power to approve or disapprove vizier's actions in the light of his own *ra'y* and *ijtihad*. The vizier of the second kind, on the other hand, is merely executing the orders of the sovereign without any independence.[124]

---

[123]Al Qur'ān, Ch. IV, ver. 59.

[124]*Ibid,* pp.. 43-51.

Ibn Taymiah:

Ibn Taymiah(661/1263-728/1328), in quite contrast to the above mentioned thinkers from Al Farabi to Ibn Jama'a, at once clung to the idealism of Shari'a, but with an accommodation to the political realities. He tried to escape from the vicious circle of Philsoshophy and reasoning in which the Muslim thinkers of his period were caught, by concentrating on Sharia and its application to the life with the religious fervour and the reforming zeal of Hanbalism.

Ibn Taymiah deduced the State from the nature of Islam, and thus, reduced the importance of the State. According to him, the 'nature of Islam' demands that there must be an organised social order where it may function properly. When the necessity of state is proved it is better to accept the authority of Allah and his Prophet as Allah orders good and forbids evil. Acceptance of all this, he holds, is obligatory upon the Mankind and these functions cannot be realised without power and authority.

He insisted upon the necessity of the authority and order, to the extent that 'the sovereign is the shadow of God on earth and sixty years under a tyrant Imam are better than a night without Imam'.[125] This statement shows that he shares his Imam, Ahmad b. Hanbal's opinion who opposed ressistance even against a tyrant ruler. In fact, Ibn Taymiah preferred stability and welfare of the community to the legitimacy and legality. He did not care whether the Imam is legal or illegal but interests of individual and congregatiomal life. He dispensed with the election and even the designation of the Caliph. According to him God designates the Imam through the infallible voice of the *ijma'*. In his theory, the centre of gravity has shifted from the *Khilafa* and *Khalifa* to the *ummah*, the community.

---

[125]Prof., Qamaruddin. *The Political Thought of Ibn Taymiyah*, pp. 27-36.

He did not insist on ideal qualifications of the Imam. In fact, he never discussed them at all. He ignored the problem of the legitimacy of incumbent in Caliphate altogether.[126]

However, in *Minhaj*, he discussed Caliph's qualifications:

1. He should be a Quraishite.
2. He should be appointed by the Consultation of the Muslims.
3. He should receive the oath of allegiance from the Muslims.
4. He should possess the quality of justice.[127]

He equally stressed upon the point that state is not a constituent of religion but a matter of practical necessity and instrument to help the cause of religion. He further stressed that the Prophet founded a state; but his regime was *Nubuwwah* (the Prophecy) not *Imamat* (the State), and he was only a Prophet not a ruler. Imamate, though not a constituent part of the faith, became one of the main functions of the Prophet in his later life and it is not external to Prophecy but inscribed and inherent in it. Further, it came into being only after the death of Prophet.[128] In fact, his main concern, here, was to refute the Shiite theory of Imamate.

For him, Islam is not merely a set of rituals but a complete way of life that can not be followed in absence of authority. Hence, he suggested the Muslims living as minorities that they must endeavour to become numerically superior to capture power.

Ibn Taymiah discussing the theory of *jihad*, observed that there are two things, Qur'an and sword that sustain Islam. He elaborated the idea further: "it is mentioned in a tradition that when a sin is

---

[126]E. I. J. Rosenthal, *Op. cit*, pp.. 51-53
[127]*Ibid*, p 84
[128] Prof., Qamaruddin. *Op. cit.*, pp. 62-63

hidden it harms only the person who commits it. But if it is open and is not condemned, it does universal harm. That is why Shari'a has enjoined war against the infidels. However, it is not obligatory until preparations have been made to fight against them."[129]

There is an inconsistency in his theory as he insists upon the importance of the state, on one hand, and undermines the sane by declaring that it is not a major issue in Islam, on the other hand. This is the consequence of his two equally important concerns namely, refuting the Shiite theory of Imamate that regards the Imamate / Caliphate as the foremost and fundamental issue of Islam, and on the other hand, stressing upon the necessity of state to enforce the Islam in toto.

Ibn Khalladun:

Ibn Khalladun presented the sociological theory of the Caliphate. He adopted a sociological approach to tackle the problem of authority in the Muslim polity, in particular and humanity in general. *Khalifa*, for him, was the choicest fruit of a God-guided and God-centred human association; it is the ideal way to the attainment of happiness in this world and hereafter. He was more concerned with Muslim society than individual Muslims. According to him the human civilisation certainly needs a state by which its affairs can be arranged in proper order.

Ibn Khalladun enumerates three kinds of states on the dual basis of government and purpose, viz. *Siyasa-e-Diniya*, i.e. government based on the Divine-Laws; *Siyasa-e-Aqliya*, i.e. government based on the law established by human reasoning; and *Siyasa-e-Madaniya,* i.e. government of the ideal state of the philosophers. According to him, the first is advantageous in this world as well as hereafter, since the legislators know what is

[129] *Ibid*, p. 37

appropriate for them and how they could get salvation hereafter. In contrast, the advantages of the second are limited merely to this world. The third, being an ideal society of the philosophers, does not require the government at all.

According to Ibn Khalladun, the Prophet was a lawgiver as well as a ruler while as the Caliph is his vicegerent, successor and ruler under the Sharia. He distinguished between the *Khilafat* and *Mulukiat* on the basis of their ultimate ends, viz. 'the welfare of the people'and 'the advantage of the ruler', respectively, though the primary source of the statutes of both may be Shari'a. However, he did not condemn this transformation, since it also serves the primary purposes of the state namely, protection of life and property. It was, for him, a natural consequence of the transformation in the psychological conditions of the people. The decline of religious knowledge strengthened the temporal component of the *Khilafa* and inevitably led to the transformation into the *Mulukiat* of the Muawia and the Umayyads.

Thus, the Islamic political theory in the above periods gradually descends from idealism to realism. Imam Hussain, by rising against the illicit authority of the usurper, Yazid, proved himself the icon of the idealism. Imam Abu Hanifa and Imam Malik, on the other hand, expressing their theory that resistance against an impostor is an obligation but with the condition of hope for success, represented the idealism with a precaution to the realistic situations of their times. Qadhi Abu Yusuf began with a purely realistic approach that followed later, passing through Shafi'i, Ahmad b. Hnabal, Ibn Taymiyya, Al Ghazali, etc. culminated into Al Mawardi's theory of Caliphate, Tusi and Ibn Jama'a's theories of *Sultanate* and *Vizierate*.

Qadhi Abu Yusuf tried to revert, by means of persuasion, to the glory of the idealistic orthodox caliphate with exception to the method of establishment of caliphate, while as Shafi'i and Ahmad

b. Hanbal and later Ibn Taymia, advocated to accept the established authority as legitimate without bothering how it originated as they were more concerned with maintainance of peace and stability than the legitimacy of the incumbent in caliphate.

Al Ghazali and Al Mawardi, on the other hand, tried to legitimise the Abbasids Caliphate, against the Fatimids and Buwahidis respectively, while as Tusi aimed at asserting the sovereignty of his Seljuk master against the claims of Abbasid-caliphs. Al Ghazali, went a step further and introduced a new method of installing the Caliph namely nomination by the Sultan or emir holding the *de facto* power.[130] Ibn Jama'a following the same line of realism, enumerated usurpation of the office through force as the third legitimate method of assuming Caliphate.[131] Al Farabi and Ibn Khalladun stand aloof by representing philosophical and sociological approaches respectively.

---

[130]E. I. J. Rosenthal, *op cit*, p. 42.

[131]*Ibid,* 45.

Ch. VI.
Muslim Political Thought in British India

In fact, the post 1857 period was a period of great turmoil and chaos for the Indian Muslims, from both, religious as well as political, point of view. With the failure in the War of Independence (1857), they had lost all their hopes of re-glorification.[132] The suppressive measures adopted by the British regime after this unsuccessful attempt ruined the Muslims in almost all aspects.[133] They faced severe economic crisis due to lost of authority, on one hand, and change of official language from Persian to English, on the other. Their traditional *Madarsa* system was replaced by the western educational system, which had no provision for Islamic religious instructions. Hence, they alienated themselves from the main stream and that resulted in lack of qualified Muslim candidates for public services. This phenomenon, in addition to the government's deliberate policy of alienation, diminished the Muslim representation in administrative machinery to a high low.[134]

Further, in 1924, Muslims faced another debacle by dissolution of Ottoman caliphate that was the last symbol, though nominal, of their political unity and sovereignty.

---

[132]See for the causes of the War, Sir Syed Ahmed Khan, *Asbāb-e Baghawat-e Hind,* & Rafiq Zakaria, *Rise of Muslims in Indian Politics,* Bombay, 1970, pp.3-7., Hence, Zakaria.

[133]See for details on Muslims' persecution by the British, Peter Hardy, *The Muslims of British India,* Cambridge, 1972, pp. 70-79. Hence, Hardy.

[134]For details see, Zakaria, pp.7-25.

The Muslim intelligentsia, at this juncture, was itself in a confused state of mind. They were divided in pro and anti British camps. Sir Syed Ahmed Khan and his followers adopted a pro-British policy. However, Maulana Abdul 'Aziz, Maulana Mahmud ul Hasan and Maulana Obaidullah Sindhi still favoured an armed struggle against the British.[135] Abdul Aziz pronounced India-under-the-British as *Dar al-Harb* and suggested the Indian Muslims to migrate to nearby Islamic countries.[136] In 1870, after collapse of Sikh-power, he revived the tradition of Shah Ismail Shaheed and Ahmed Barelvi (1786-1831), re-organised the military potential of *Mujahideen,* in the North-Western province, and collided with the British but in vain.[137]

At the advent of the twentieth century, Maulana Mahmud ul Hasan, chief of the *Dar ul-'ulūm* Deoband, strived to follow the *jihad* tradition of *Mujahidīn.* He founded an underground movement, which was later known as *Reshmi Rumal Tehreek.* He planned to strike the British through the Khyber Pass with the possible help of Muslim countries like Afghanistan, Iran and Turkey. In 1918, he sent his most trusted disciple, Obaidullah Sindhi, to Afghanistan in order to establish contacts with the Emir of Afghanistan and Shah of Iran as well as to consolidate the unorganised *Mujahideen,* who were impatient to strike the British. In the same year, he himself left for Hejaz to seek military help from Turkish government. Anwar Pasha, the Turkish War Minister, appreciated his programme and promised to extend help in this

---

[135]For details see, Hardy, p. 84.

[136]Qadhi Mohd. Aslam Saif, *Tahreek-e Ahl-e Hadith, Tareekh Ke Aainay mein,* Al-Kitab International, New Delhi,1996, p.252; See for detail discussion on *dar ul-harb*, *Ibid,* pp. 109-115.

[137]Aziz Ahmed, *Islamic Modernism in India and Pakistan, 1857-1964*, London, 1967, p. 20. Hence, Aziz Ahmed.

endeavour. Meanwhile, Obaidullah Sindhi established a Government-in-exile with several associates of the '*Ghadar Movement*' at Kabul. But, the entire plan collapsed as the British succeeded in arresting Mahmud ul Hasan along with his followers at Mecca itself, from where they were sent to Malta for imprisonment.[138]

Nanotawi and Deoband

The bulk of *Ulama* were of the view that the salvation of the Indian Muslims lay in a renewed and vigorous effort to revive and rejuvenate Islam.[139] They were more concerned of the intellectual advent of the western ideas than her political domination. They were anxious about the existence of Islam and Muslims in this land. Maulana Qasim Nanotawi (1832-1880), an*Alim* of a high repute, believed that imparting religious education among the Muslims was the need of the hour lest they would perish. Though, he was not against the modern sciences, he thought that the government has already taken up the task and established the institutions of modern and scientific learning, while there was no such arrangement for disseminating theological knowledge.[140] Hence, he along with Maulana Haji Imdadullah Muhajir Makki and Maulana Rashid Ahmed Gangohi decided, in 1867, to establish a seminary at Deoband exclusively for religious education, unadulterated by western influence. Hence, modern sciences and English could not form a part in the curriculum. Being products of the Waliullahi

---

[138]Ziya ul Hasan Faruqi, *Deoband School and the Demand for Pakistan*, Bombay, 1967, pp. 59-62., Hence, Faruqi.

[139]Zakaria, p. 26.

[140]For details on introduction of modern education by the British see, Hardy, pp. 90-91 & Wm. T. De Bary, *Sources of Indian Tradition,* New York, 1958, pp. 35-37, Hence, De Bary.

school[141] they were more concerned about the conservation of the tradition of their school and the *Hanafi maslak.*

However, one may note that the objectives of the establishment of Deoband were not that simple.[142] All the three founders were not just academic luminaries of high excellence but active participants in the War of Independence at Shamli as well.[143] In fact, there was a profound underlying aim, namely re-gaining the theo-political glory of the past. For them, in fact, Shamli and Deoband were two facets of the same coin. The difference lies only in weapons. At Shamli resort was made to arms, here at Deoband they made a start to achieve the same goal through intellectual and peaceful means.[144] The presence of physical training of quasi-military nature, that led the people to remark sarcastically that it was rather a *Madarsa-e Harbia* instead of a *Madarsa-e Arabia,*

---

[141]Most of the Muslim Movements of British India, many of whom were antagonistic to each other such as *Ahnaf* and *Ahl-e-Hadith*, surprisingly trace back their origin in Shah Waliullah's writings. His theo-political thought keeps the Islam alive in the Indian sub-continent. He wanted the Muslim society to return to the Prophet-era for the political unity of the then Muslim rulers. (Sayed Riaz Ahmad, *Maulana Maududi and Islamic state*, People's Publishing House, Lahore 1976, p. 15).

[142]Mawlana Mahmud al-Hasan's remarks are crucial in this regard. He questioned, when he was suggested by the administration of *Dar al-'Uloom* to keep away from politics, "Did our revered teacher (Nanotawi) founded this *madarsah* for mere educational purposes? It was founded in my presence and, as far as I know, one of its main objects was to compensate for the losses in 1857. Those interested only in education are free to do as they like but I stand for those objects which the founder of the *Dar al-'Uloom* had in view and for whose achievement he worked hard". (Faruqi, p. 59, n. 1)

[143]*Ibid,* p. 21.

[144]*Ibid,* p. 23.

envisages the minds of its founders.[145] However, later in course of time it became a neglected aspect of the curriculum as the people at Deoband, with exception of few, had forgotten the real aim of its founding father.

Syed Ahmed Khan and Aligarh Tehreek

On the other side, Sir Syed Ahmed Khan (1817-1898), who was also a product of the traditional education, had radical views with regard to the nature and curriculum of education among Muslims. He had a strong belief that the key for salvation of Muslim community lies in their learning of English language, acquirig modern education and adopting western culture and civilisation. He insisted upon Muslims that they must abandon all those habits and beliefs that were in contrast to the western culture, civilisation, morality, or modern sciences. He pronounced that the real Islam would not be an impediment to the proposed modernisation as the *wahy* and natural laws are identical and connote the words and works of the Almighty respectively. The words of God i.e. Qur'ãn must be in harmony with the works of God i.e. Nature. Hence, the Qur'ãn cannot contradicts the law of nature. Similarly, *wahy* and reason are identical. *Wahy* operates as natural instinct in lower forms of life while the reason as a revelation-instinct operates in scientific investigation.[146] Hence, Qur'ãnic Eschatology, Angelology, Demonology and Cosmology cannot contradict to scientific actuality and must be interpreted in its terms. He considered *Jihad* as a defensive warfare and slavery as the product of historical Islam, not the real and revealed

---

[145]*Ibid,* pp. 30-37.

[146]Aziz Ahmed, pp. 42-43 & S. M. Ikram, *Indian Muslims and the Partition of India,* New Delhi, p. 55., Hence, Ikram.

Islam.[147]

His approach was purely materialistic and he was concerned with betterment of the mundane life of Muslims. For this sake, he was ready to interpret the Qur'ãn according to his modernistic and naturalistic point of view. In order to tune the Qur'ãnic verses with the western criteria he formulated his own fifteen principles of exegesis. He advocated that all Muslims have the right of a symbolic or analytical interpretation of the Qur'ãn. He divided the Qur'ãnic verses into two kinds, essential and symbolic. The former constituting the irreducible minimum of the faith, while the later being open to interpretations in accordance with exigencies of the prevailing circumstances, different from those of Arabia in the seventh century.[148] The bases of interpretation, said Sir Syed, were to be the underlying principles *(usūl)* and not the minutiae *(furū')* derived therefrom. Similarly, the Qur'ãnic verses referring to the specific historical situations cannot be a basis for interpretation.[149] To rid with the unaccommodating *ahadith* he, like Goldziher and Schacht, challenged the authenticity of all the classical collections, including *Sahih Bukhari* and *Sahih Muslim.*[150]

Further, for the sake of developing cordial relations between Christianity and Islam he has written two books, *Tabaiin al-Kalam* and *Risala der Ta'am ahl al-Kitab,* in which he advocated that the Muslims should remove the social barriers with regard to the

---

[147]Sir Syed regarded the Prophet's expeditions as a defensive warfare-mechanism. *Ibid,* p. 50.

[148]Sir Syed, on this basis, pronounced that the simple interest drawn from banks or government institutions is permissible. *Ibid,* pp. 45 & 52-54., However, astonishingly he supported *purdah* among the Muslim women. (Zakaria, p. 244)

[149]Aziz Ahmed, p. 42.

[150]*Ibid,* p. 49.

Christians.[151] While dealing all these, he was daring enough to criticise the British policy of discrimination against the Indians. He left the *Agra Durbar* unattended when he noticed that the chairs for Indian guests were arranged on a lower level to those of Europeans.[152]

However, Sir Syed concentrated upon the popularisation of western education and social reforms among the Muslims. After a thorough analysis, he concluded that the root cause of all the backwardness and sufferings of the Muslims was their abhorrence to the English language, western education and sciences. He realised that if Muslims were not acquainted with the modern education their condition will not be improved and they could not get an honourable position amongst the nations of the world. In 1864, he founded the Scientific Society for introduction of modern sciences among the Indian Muslims. He started with the establishment of a modern school at Ghazipur and encouraged the others to establish such institutions at the district level. However, he, unlike his predecessor Nanotawi, stressed upon English and modern sciences. He caused the translation of useful English books into Urdu. However, his great achievement in the field of education is the establishment of Anglo-Muhammadan Oriental College in 1874, at Aligarh on the model of Cambridge University with English as the medium of instruction. It aimed at the scientific education, broad mindedness, liberalisation of ideas, and a pragmatic approach to politics. This college in course of time developed into Aligarh Muslim University.[153]

These endeavours produced a small but talented intelligentsia

---

[151]Zakaria, pp. 237-238.

[152]S. M. Ikram, Modern Muslim India and the Birth of Pakistan, Delhi, 1991, p. 42., Hence, Modern Muslim India.

[153]Aziz Ahmed, pp. 34-38., see for details, Ikram, pp. 31, 37-40.

that contributed much in development of political consciousness among the Muslims and created dynamics in the fossilised society. It provided the leadership for Muslims to check the growing influence of the Congress. Moreover, the neo-elite, who had little sympathy towards Islam and its tenets, later played an active role in Pakistan movement as they believed in Muslim Nationalism with respect to the Indian subcontinent.

On the political front, Sir Syed was convinced that the British rule over India has been beneficial and a Divine blessing to the Indians, especially to the Muslims. Hence, he remained loyal towards the British through out his life and preached the same. He condemned the efforts to present the Mutiny of 1857 as a Muslim revolt and started a magazine, *The Loyal Muhammadans of India,* to correct the false impression of British officials.[154] His loyalism can be divided in three phases. From 1859 to 1870, he aimed to convince, on one hand, the British government that as long as the Indian Muslims enjoyed the liberty to perform their religious rituals there could be no theological case for them to rise against the British,[155] and, on the other, the Muslim community that the British rule over India was in their interest. In the second phase, from 1870 to 1884, his objective was to check the advent of pan-Islamism, which he considered as a dangerous political adventurism. In the third phase, from 1887 to 1898, he led the Muslims towards political separatism. He, on the basis of Urdu-Hindi controversy and the communal riots that followed, concluded that these two

---

[154] Ikram, p. 30., see also, Hardy, pp.84-85.

[155] Lord Mayo, wrote a letter, dt.30th May 1871, to W.W. Hunter to write a book on the burning question that "Are the India Muslims bound by their religion to rebel against the Queen? (Hardy, p. 85, see also, pp. 62-70)

nations could not be united into a composite nation.[156] He succeeded in the first and third phase of his loyalism, but on the question of pan-Islamism he failed to attract the Muslim intelligentsia as well as masses.[157]

In 1884, with regard to the self-government, he suggested a political pattern based on triangular, Hindu, Muslim, and British, participation. He was convinced that if either of the Hindus or the Muslims rule the country, peace couldn't be maintained; therefore, the British rule is inevitable to retain the peaceful co-existence of all the communities in India. He was very critical of the Congress and always considered it as a Hindu organisation. He was afraid of any political alliance with the Hindus. In his view, it could lead only to the eventual domination and subjugation of the Muslim minority to the Hindu majority. Therefore, he opposed the Congress' stance to appease the minority, in the form of Khilafat Movement. He reacted sharply when the Congress elected a Muslim, Badruddin Tayyabji, as its president. He condemned it as the beginning of erosion in Muslim community, which was numerically in minority, educationally backward, politically immature, and economically weak.[158] He had certain reservations regarding the association with the Congress; firstly, he was afraid of the cultural dominance of the Hindus in the Congress that association with such an organisation would cause loss of identity for the Muslims and eventually they would absorb, like the Buddhists and Jains, into the Hindu community. Secondly, that the Congress' anti-British attitude would ruin the Muslim community again as it happened after the Mutiny of 1857. Hence, he pronounced that the Muslim's alliance with the Congress would

---

[156]Zakaria, p. 82.
[157]Aziz Ahmed, p. 33.
[158]*Ibid,* p. 34.

cause 'a loss to this world as well as hereafter'.[159] He founded two organisations, United Indian Patriotic Association in 1888, and Anglo-Oriental Defence Association in 1894 to counteract the Congress' influence on Indians, in general and Muslims in particular.[160]

In brief, Sir Syed's Naturalism rejected or reinterpreted all those elements in Islam that contradicts the modern science or western culture and civilisation; for this sake, he strived to rationalise the minutiae of dogma and thereby liberalise the Islamic law. Thus, in this endeavour he disowned three-fourth of Islam. His Rationalist speculation, in which he was close to the Mu'tazilites, and loyalist Occidentalism can be summed up in the following six points:

- A rationalistic approach to Islam;
- A readjustment of Islamic traditions and customs in accordance with the changing times, i.e. according to western criterion;
- An active interest in the history and literature of Islam;
- A new approach to life that was Islamic in its roots but adjustable with the modern requirements, i.e. western civilisation;
- A better understanding of the Christians and their culture and civilisation; and
- A loyalism towards the British combined with Muslim separatism.[161]

Though, Sir Syed did not formally establish any organisation,

---

[159]Zakaria, p. 84.

[160]For more details on these association see, *ibid,* pp. 66-70 & 82-85.

[161]*Ibid,* p. 240.

his theo-socio-political endeavours has been generally referred as Aligarh Movement'.

Chiragh Ali and Rationalism

Chiragh Ali (1844-1895), a radical disciple of Syed Ahmed Khan who called himself as Mu'tazili,[162] went a step ahead of his master. He considered the Prophet primarily as a reformer, who replaced the Arabian superstition by monotheism, elevated the moral standards of Arabs and improved the lot of women. He, in unequivocal words, repudiated the authenticity of the *Ahadith* and rejected *Ijma'* as a source of law. He expressed reservations with regard to the authenticity of the traditional sources of law.[163] He also suggested that too much sanctity should not be attached to the Prophet, his words and practices.[164]

Chiragh Ali envisaged that the Qur'ãn is full of references to nature and the laws of nature. He endeavoured to identify *Mutlaq*, i.e. absolute and *Muqayyad* i.e. conditional verses in Qur'ãn and formulated the principle that an 'absolute' verse should be interpreted in the light of a 'conditional' one when the situation and the ruling are parallel. According to him, Islam exists as a religion distinct from a social system, though, Muslims in various phases of their history confused the individual or cumulative experience of their social systems with the Qur'ãn. Islamic jurisprudence was essentially a reflection of such social experiences of ninth and tenth centuries. It may be still practicable in fossilised and static Muslim societies. But, in countries like India, Algeria and Turkey, which have been exposed to west, some of its sections become outdated and require re-writing. In such countries a new legal theory has to

---

[162] *Ibid,* p. 242.
[163] Aziz Ahmed, pp. 57-61.
[164] Zakaria, p. 242.

be evolved to bring comprehensive legislative changes in the inherited traditional law, to eliminate outdated, inefficient, unprogressive and inhuman features in legal institutions. Similarly, in the Ottoman Empire, the marriage and divorce laws had to be reformed and equality of all citizens, Muslim and non-Muslim, had to be established. He disowned the legal disabilities against non-Muslims as having no real theological basis. He also considered Jihad as a defensive mechanism irrelevant to the development of modernist Islam.[165] For him, all references of the Qur'ãn with regard to the sword was false, meant only to malign Islam as the Qur'ãn itself declared in unequivocal words that 'there is no compulsion in religion'.[166]

He, in his '*the Proposed Political, Legal and Social Reforms in the Ottoman Empire and other Muhammadan States*', pleaded for religion-politics dichotomy as the Prophet never combined the church and state into one.[167]

With regard to the politics, Chiragh Ali had remained a staunch loyalist in the tradition of his master. He generally opposed the Muslim participation in the Congress as well as their subscription to the view of pan-Islamism. However, he was sympathetic with certain aspects of nationalist movement, such as inter-communal harmony and peaceful coexistence with Hindus.[168]

Titu Mir and Tariqa-e-Muhammadiya

Titu Mir (1782-1831), a reformist turned rebel, founded a movement, *Tariqa-e-Muhammadiya*, in Bengal. This was in fact a socio-religious reformist movement that soon acquired the

---

[165]Aziz Ahmed, pp. 59-62.

[166]Zakaria, p. 242.

[167]*Ibid,* p. 242.

[168] Aziz Ahmed, p. 65.

character of an armed rebellion against British due to the laters continuous support to the oppressive landlords.

Titu initially preached against polytheism (*shirk*) and innovations (*bid'aat*) but in a short span of time found himself in the midst of a confrontation between him and local Zamindars and English Indigo planters as he resisted their oppressive measures too. He petitioned before British but in vain. Then he preferred to take the matter into his own hands and formed a Mujahid force and trained them in *lathi* and other indigenous arms. British authorities took serious note of these activities and sent offensives against them. Titu bravely defeated at least three of such offensives but could not sustain for a long time before the well equipped British forces and martyred on 19th November 1831 after five days of fierce battle.[169]

Haji Shariatullah and Faraedhi Tehreek

Haji Shariatullah(1781-1840) after returning from Mecca, where he availed the opportunity to learn for twenty years from Shaikh Tahir Sombal, an authority of Hanafi School, launched another movement, *Faraedhi Tehreek*, in Bengal, to bring the Bengali Muslims to the true path of Islam. The term *Faraedhi* is derived from '*fardh*', i.e. obligatory duties enjoined by Allah. However, Haji Shariatullah interpreted the term in a broader sense to include all religious duties enjoined by the Qur'ãn & Sunnah.

Bengali Muslims, while ignoring the real Islam, had been indulging in several un-Islamic customs, rituals and ceremonies. Shariatullah laid utmost emphasis on the five fundamentals of Islam; insisted on the complete acceptance and strict observation of

---

[169]'Titu Mir', *Wikipedia*, Electronic edn, 2008 cited to Rabiya Khatoon, *Titumirer Bansher Kella*, 1981.

pure monotheism; and condemned all deviations from Islam, such as saint-worship, undue reverence to *Peer*, as *shirk*, polytheism and *Chhuttee*, *Puttee*, *Chilla*, *Shabgasht*, *Fatiha, Milad*, *Urs*, *Taziah* as *Bid'at*, i.e. sinful innovations. He laid stress on justice, social equality, and the universal brotherhood of Muslims. He used the terms *ustaad* and *shagird* to denote his relation with his disciples.

On the political side, Haji Shariatullah regarded British rule as harmful to the Islam and Muslims. He pronounced that the absence of a legitimate Muslim caliph or his representative in Bengal deprived the Bengali Muslims the privilege of holding congregational and Friday prayers.

This movement spread with extraordinary zeal in of Dhaka, Faridpur, Bakerganj, Mymensingh, Tippera, Chittagong, Noakhali districts and the adjacent province of Assam. He was expelled by the police in 1831 from his centre, Ramnagar or Nayabari. The continuous clashes with the Hindu landlords and European indigo planters converted the movement gradually into a pre-dominant socio-economic programme. He ordered his disciples to resist illegal cess and restriction upon cow slaughter. To rid off Shariatullah, the Hindu land-lords, in 1837, accused him of attempting to set up a kingdom on the lines of Titu Meer. They also brought numerous cases, with the help of European indigo planters against the Faraedhis. He was arrested by the police several times for allegedly causing agrarian disturbances in Faridpur.

On Shariathullah's demise his son Muhsinuddin Ahmad alias Dudu Miyan presided over the movement and under his leadership it assumed an agrarian character. He organised the oppressed peasantry against the oppressive landlords. The landlords and indigo planters tried to contain Dudu Miyan by implicating him in false cases but in vain due to his popularity with the peasantry.

The initial victories of Dudu Miyan added impetus to the Faraedhi movement and attracted not only Muslims but the Hindus and native Christians also. They also sought Dudu Miyan's protection against the oppressive landlords.[170]

Al Qanunji and Ahl-e-Hadith

Muhammad Siddiq Hasan Khan al Qanunji (1832-1890) founded an Islamic puritan movement, *Ahl-e-Hadith*, in the late 19th century on the ideas of Shah Waliullah (d. 1763), Syed Ahmad Shaheed (d. 1831) and Qaḍi Ash-Shaukani (d. 1832). Its aim was to bring religious reform by denouncing *Taqlid*, i.e. the following of any particular Imam amongst the four Imams of *Ahl-e-Sunnah*, as *bid'a*, i.e. sinful innovation. They were nicknamed as Indian Wahabis as ideologically they were akin with Muhammad b. Abdul Wahab of Najad.

Sadiq Hasan married the third Begum of Bhopal, Shah Jahan (reigned 1868-1901), that made his position strong enough to combat the traditional Indian '*ulama*, who were Hanafites. He compiled more than 200 books in Arabic, Persian and Urdu. Further, he established a far-reaching network to sell his books and buy of others for him. This challenges the common view that the nineteenth century India was just a periphery which did not participated in the intellectual developments and the trends of Islamic centres.[171]

Shibili N'umani and Historical Glorification

Shibili N'umani (1857-1914) strived to establish a synthesis between the extreme orthodoxy of traditional *'ulama* and extremist modernism and naturalism of western educated intelligentsia. He

---

[170]"Faraezi Tehreek", *Wikipedia*, Online edn, 2008.
[171]*Ibid*, cited to Claudia Preckel, *The Begums of Bhopal*, Rolibooks, New Delhi.

approved of English education and modernisation of certain social institutions, but to the extent that it did not harm the religious foundations of Islam. He discarded the superfluous and the ridiculous elements of the Muslim society while adhered to the essentials of the faith.

He was the driving force behind the establishment of *Nadwat al-'Ulama* at Lucknow as a synthesis between the orthodoxy of Deoband and modernism of Aligarh. He admired many things in western civilisation and did not mind to borrow the ideas and institutions from Europe, or for that matter, from anywhere if those were absolutely essential for the regeneration of Islam. However, he was to measure the western ideas and values by the Islamic yardstick. Hence, he disagreed with Sir Syed in many of his theological interpretations. For instance, he, in quite contrast to Sir Syed, considered reason as the handmaid of religion.[172]

With regard to the treatment of non-Muslim subjects, he suggested liberal measures. He discarded discriminatory practices against *dhimmis* in erstwhile Islamic states as the personal attitude of the rulers, not essentially Islamic.[173]

Shibili created the tradition of Islamic historiography in Urdu with a profound aim to revive the glories of Islam, at least in the hearts and minds of the new generation. He synthesised between the traditional Islamic disciplines of chronicles and hagiography and the western discipline of objective analysis. He appreciated the Orientalists' efforts of investigation of cultural and religious resources to establish a historical and scientific perspective to the study of Islam.[174]

Shibili has taken the refuge of history with two fold aims:

---

[172]Zakaria, pp. 251-253.
[173]Aziz Ahmed, pp. 81-83.
[174]*Ibid,* p. 78.

firstly, to bring the Muslim community out of dismay and gloom that became its destiny since the unsuccessful War of 1857, by reminding their past glories; secondly, to convince the *'ulama* that several ideas and institutions have been borrowed from different sources alien to Islam during the earliest period of Islam, even in the reign of orthodox caliphs. And he succeeded to a considerable extent in both his objectives.

Obaidullah Sindhi and Hijrat Movement

Maulana Obaidullah Sindhi (d. 1944), a convert from Sikhism and a prominent disciple of Maulana Mahmud al-Hasan (1851-1920) was a real dynamic. He, besides taking part in the *Reshmi Rumal Tehreek,* initiated another movement called as *Hijrat* Movement. It declared India as *dar al-harb* and encouraged the Muslims to migrate to Muslim countries. At Kabul, he established a government-in-exile with associates of the '*Ghadar Tehreek*'.

On the political side, he, in the tradition of Deoband, accepted the composite nation theory as a practical solution for gaining independence, but to a far more restricted extent than the *Deobandi-'ulama*. He was first to develop the idea of linguistic nationalities in India. He envisaged free India as a confederation of linguistic and cultural nationalities. Among the leading theories, Socialism attracted him most. Astonishingly, he attributed this idea to the certain writings of Shah Waliullah. In his view, Islam was basically and inherently Socialistic. He has seen the Communist revolution in the USSR as close to Islam. He envisaged that the Muslims should evolve a religious basis for themselves to arrive at the economic justice at which communism aims but cannot fully achieve. *Jihad*, for him, was the basis of organisation of Islamic social revolution. However, this aim can also be achieved by peaceful means. He identified victory of Islamic social revolution on social scale as fulfilment of God's blessings on earth.

The difference, in his view, between the social revolution preached by Islam and communism was that the former believes in God while the later denies Him. He connotes the Qur'ãnic concept of *Jama'a* with Communist concept of revolutionary party.[175]

Muhammad Ali Jauhar & Khilafat Movement

Muhammad Ali Jauhar (1879-1930) was a real Pan-Islamist in action. His loyalty towards Islam was beyond the national considerations. At the onslaught of European powers over the Ottoman Empire he represented the anguish and anxiety of Indian Muslims regarding the fate of Caliphate, which had been regarded as the symbol of secular power and unity of Muslims worldwide. During the First World War, he requested the Allies to help the Turks to keep them away from the Germans. Despite these appeals, the Britain wrested several territories from Turkey, which shocked the Indian Muslims. Yet, they believed that they could pressurise the British and this could bring good to their Turkish brethren. Hence, they, under the leadership of Muhammad Ali, caused, in 1920, the *Khilafat* movement.

Congress, at that moment, was keen to attract Muslim support. In fact, it had been since its inception, in 1885, striving to draw the Muslims towards it to cast off the Hindu colour and to present itself as a true representative body of all the Indians. The *Khilafat* question provided an excellent opportunity to it. Hence, it decided to take the matter as its own. The entire nation under the dual leadership of Gandhi and Jauhar stood united for the Turkish cause. However, this alliance could not last long as the Muslims turned hostile towards the Congress again when Gandhi ji called off the non-cooperation movement on the excuse of infiltration of violence

---

[175]Aziz Ahmed, pp. 195-201.

into it, while Muslim masses, including Jauhar, considered it as a lame excuse and moved further away from the Congress. The *Khilafat* movement hung up until the Turks themselves abolished the Caliphate in 1924. Muhammad Ali died in London where he was to attend the first Round Table Conference.176

Iqbal and Pan-Islamism

Muhammad Iqbal (1875-1938), the poet, philosopher, theo-political thinker and an intellectual leader of the Muslim intelligentsia, was in fact an embodiment of the orthodox Orientalism and modern Occidentalism. He was convinced that a reconstruction of shariah had become essential due to the revolutionary changes in modern times. The traditional interpretations were good for the times in which they were made but in the context of the modern conditions, they become obsolete. He felt the need of a great faqih who could interpret Islam correctly in the light of new developments. According to some reports he put his hopes on Maududi.

Iqbal suggested certain valuable reforms as an immediate concern. For instance, the proper protection of the rights of women and their education. He supported *purdah* and polygamy and condemned wasteful expenditure in Muslim-ceremonies. He pursued the Muhammadan Educational Conference to establish a Reforms Section under its auspices.

In the field of education, Iqbal stressed upon the industrial education. In his view, there was no hope of progress without it.[177] However, he opposed neither traditional nor modern education.

Iqbal's contribution to the legal thought of Islam was his

---

[176]De Bary, pp. 216-220.
[177]Zakaria, pp. 259-262.

advocacy for the enlargement of the scope and authority of *Ijma'* and *Ijtihad.* He envisaged that the power of *Ijtihad* should be taken from the individuals and vested in a representative assembly of various schools of Islamic Jurisprudence. The consensus reached in such a body, for him, was *Ijma'*. In his view, Muslim law can be amended to meet the needs of a modern society, as it was not a sacrosanct element of Islamic faith. For him, the fossilisation of Islamic Law under the guise of *Fiqahi mazahibs* (Schools of jurisprudence) is an artificial phenomenon that can be corrected by a return to *Ijtihad* on the basis of other three sources of Islamic Law, viz. Qur'an, Hadith and Ijma'.[178]

In his view, Islam is an ethical ideal with certain kind of polity by which it aimed to create a social structure regulated by a legal system and functioned thrpough specific ethical ideals.[179] He was against religion-politics dichotomy as he was convinced that in Islam there is no such duality between spirit and matter, consequently, between Church and State. According to him, both were organic to each other. He rejected the idea of limiting the religion to the private sphere of the individual life. He, in his poetic style, envisaged that the Prophet created a social order which provides the fundamentals of a polity with implicit legal concepts. Therefore, the religious ideal of Islam was organically so intervowened with its social order that rejection of the one will results the rejection of the other *ipso facto*. He disapproved the idea of retaining Islam as an ethical ideal but rejecting it as a polity in favour of national polities. He was against the establishment of national states among Muslims and considered it as against the universal spirit of Islam. On the contrary, he advocated al-Afghani's Pan-Islamism. In his narrative poem, *Jawed Nama,* he

---

[178]Aziz Ahmed, pp.154-155.
[179]*Ibid,* p. 160.

presented his ideal Islamic state in the words of al-Afghani.

Nevertheless, he did not see any contradiction between pan-Islamism and demand for Pakistan as he considered the Indian case a distinct one. He rejected the idea of a composite nation of Hindus and Muslims on the basis that establishment of a state on national considerations that involved a displacement of Islamic principles, was unthinkable for a Muslim. He condemned Maulana Hussein Ahmed Madani for his statement that a composite nation could be constituted in India on the basis of homeland.[180] He pointed out that in modern terminology homeland was a political concept that contradicted with Islam. In his view, the moral consciousness, emotional and psychological homogeneity that was required to constitute the essence of nation was not present in India. Thus, he intentionally or unintentionally played a typical role in the genesis of the very idea of Pakistan.[181] He suggested an autonomous province comprising of Muslims majority provinces of the subcontinent under an Indian federation to solve the communal problem. In his view, the fact of diversity within the Indian nation has to be recognised lest it would lead to intensify the inner tensions between these two communities.[182] He writes:

> "I would like to see the Punjab, North-West Frontier Province, Sind and Baluchistan amalgamated into a single State. Self government within British Empire, or without British the British Empire, the formation of a consolidated North-West Indian Muslim state appears to me to be the final destiny of the Muslims, at least of North-West India."[183]

---

[180]Iqbāl, Tasadduq Hussein Tāj, ed. *Madhamīn-e-Iqbāl*. pp. 180-196.
[181]Aziz Ahmed, pp. 156-163.
[182]De Bary, pp. 211-215.
[183]*Ibid,* p. 215.

Later this idea, in the hands of Jinnah, eventually led to the Pakistan Resolution for a sovereign Muslim State.

Maulana Ilyas and Tablighi Jamat

Maulana Muhammad Ilyas Kandhalavi (1885-1944) founded the Tablighi Jamat, in late 1920s, at Mewat as an apolitical and purely missionary movement. According to him, he inspired by a dream during the Hajj in 1926. Tabligh in Arabic means ‘to convey (the message)’ and Tablighi Jamat strives to revive this duty which they consider as one of the primary duties of Muslims.

Maulana Ilyas put forward the slogan, ‘*Aye Musalmano! Musalman Bano*’, (‘O Muslims! Become (real) Muslims’). This expressed the prime focus of Tablighi Jamat. The aim of *Tabligh* has been renewing Muslim society by reminding basic obligations of Islam, especially the prayer, to the Muslims. He enunciatd a six-point formulae to become a true Muslim. The points were:

1. Firm belief in the *Kalimah*;
2. Concentration and Devotion in prayer;
3. *'Ilm* (knowledge) and *Dhikr* (to remind the God);
4. *Ikram-e-Muslim* (respect towards Muslims);
5. *Ikhlas-e-Niyyat* (good intention);
6. *Dawat wa Tabligh* (conveying of the message and propagation)

Maulana Ilyas was a prominent member of the Deobandi movement and throughout Tabligh’s history there has been a close association between the two, although, Tablighi Jamat does not see itself as Deobandi and vice versa.

Tabligh was formed at a time when there was a general apprehension that Indian Muslims have been losing their distinct identity to the majority Hindu culture.

After Malulana Ilyas’ demise (d. 1944) his son Maulana

Muhammad Yusuf Kandhalvi (1917-65) became the second *Amir* followed by Maulana Inaam ul Hasan (1965-95).

Now, in India, there is a *shura* consisting of two leaders, Maulana Zubair ul Hasan and Maulana Sa'ad Kandhalvi. In Pakistan the duties of the Ameer are being served by Haji Abdul Wahab. Maulana Zakariya Kandhalvi was also among the leading personalities of the Tabligh, as he compiled the famous book *Fazail-e-Amal*, that later became basic literature of the Tablighi.[184]

Inayatullah Mashriqi & Khaksar Tehreek

Inayatullah Mashriqi (1888-1963) was the founder of *Khaksar Tehreek*. He was concerned with the conflict within various religions. He believed that conflict among various religions is not possible as the same God could not have sent conflicting messages. If any conflict is existed it means that the religion and the messenger are ingenune or it is adulterated by its followers. He, after an analytical study, concluded that the teachings of all the prophets were closely linked with evolution of the mankind as a single and united species in contrast to species of animals. On this basis, he declared that the Science of Religions was essentially the science of collective evolution of mankind; all prophets came to unite mankind, not to divide it; the basic law of all faiths is the law of unification and consolidation of the entire humanity.

After resigning from British service, Mashriqi laid the foundation of the *Khaksar Tehreek* in 1930. He played a role in directing the Muslims towards the independence. Mashriqi was repeatedly imprisoned, along with his family and a large number of *Khaksars*. He in 1938 announced 14 points charter in which the

---

[184]"Tabligh Jamat" *Wikipedia*, on Net 2008; Alex Alexiev, 'Tablighi Jamāt: Jihad's Stealthy Legions', in *Middle East Quarterly*, Winter 05, vol. XXII. No.1.

first point reads:

> "We *Khaksars* are determined to establish, by destroying all sectarian feelings and religious bigotry (but keeping religion intact), an egalitarian, non-partisan and tolerant order which would ensure a fair deal to all nations and their rightful growth, and which will be based on virtue, struggle, action and supreme justice." [185]

In this juncture, the two centres of Muslim education and thought, viz. Deoband and Aligarh, which were, in the words of Obaid Ullah Sindhi, 'the two facets of the theological heritage of Waliullahi tradition',[186] presented two different and extremely antagonistic approaches.

Azad & Madani and Composite Nation Theory

There was, on one hand, the Composite Nation Theory or United Indian Nationalism, presented by Indian National Congress and seconded by *Jami'yat-e-'Ulama-e-Hind,* founded in 1919, by the *'Ulama* of Deoband, Nadwah and Firangi Mahal under the leadership of Maulana Hussein Ahmed Madani.[187] Maulana Rashid Ahmed Gangohi, Maulana Mahmood al-Hasan and Maulana 'Obaidullah Sindhi, under the impression that an armed struggle

---

[185]"Mashriqui", *Wikipaedia*, Electronic edn, 2008

[186]Aziz Ahmed, p. 104.

[187]It is noteworthy that a small section of the '*ulama-e* Deoband was against the composite nation theory and collaboration with the Congress. Mawlana Ashraf 'Ali Thanawi (1863-1943) was the leader of this group. He along with Mawlana Shabbir Ahmed 'Uthmani and few other *'ulama-e*-Deoband defected from the *Jami'yat al-'Ulama-e Hind* and established *Jami'yat al-'Ulama-e Islam,* in 1946. They with the blessings of Mr. Jinnah counteracted the formers' activities. However, the bulk of the Deobandi '*Ulama* were against the demand for Pakistan. Faruqi, pp. 102-103, n. 4.

was inappropriate at that time, also subscribed to that theory.[188] This theory advocates that the Hindus and Muslims of the Indian subcontinent together constitute a composite nation as they share the same homeland. Hence, they should live united under single government in a single sovereign state, by a federal arrangement, with their respective religious identities.[189] It considers the homeland as the very core of the nationalism. Hussein Ahmed pronounced:

> "We, the inhabitants of India, in so far as we are Indians, have one thing in common and that is our Indianness which remains unchanged in spite of our religious and cultural differences. As the diversities in our appearances, individual qualities and personal traits and colour and stature do not affect our common humanness, similarly, our religious and cultural differences do not interfere with our common associations with our homeland. - - - - - This is what I mean by the '*Muttahidah Qawmiyat*'."[190]

Maulana Abul Kalam Azad (1888-1958), a man of the Congress by conviction, provided the theological basis for this theory. He connoted the situation in India with that of Medina immediately after the *Hijrah*. According to him, in the Covenant, concluded between the Prophet and the people of Medina, Muslims as well as Jews and Pagans were described as a single community. He presented it as a precedent to constitute the composite nation of all the Indians irrespective of their religion.[191]

It was obvious that the Jami'yat had been advocating geographical considerations, instead of religious affiliation, as the

---

[188] Aziz Ahmed, p. 190.
[189] *Ibid,* p.104.
[190] *Ibid,* pp. 103-104.
[191] *Ibid,* p. 189.

basis for the constitution of a nation and thereby repudiating the very idea of Pakistan. Jami'yat's anxiety with the demand for Pakistan was three-fold;

- Firstly, it was suspicious about the British designs.[192]
- Secondly, it was anxious about the safety and security of the Muslims left in India as minorities after the division.[193]
- Thirdly, it was thinking with a missionary viewpoint that the division will surely cease, or at least impede, their objective of propagation of Islam among the Hindus.[194]

In this regard Maulana Hussein Ahmed Madani wrote:

> "And Islam being a missionary religion, it is its duty, so far as possible, to absorb others in itself, not to reject them. This is why we should not hate our neighbouring peoples even if they hate us, if they call us unclean and impure."[195]
>
> "The great object of an over-all spread of Islam in the whole of India cannot be realised by appealing to passions of hatred and antagonism. It is the non-Muslims who are the field of action for the *'tabligh'* of Islam and form the raw material for this splendid activity. Today, by propagating hatred towards the Hindus, this field is being closed and this material wasted. It is contrary to the universal message of our great Prophet."[196]
>
> "Our object is to bridge the gulf of hatred, which is being created by the protagonists of the scheme of

---

[192]*Ibid,* pp.106-111.
[193]*Ibid,* pp. 111-114.
[194]*Ibid,* pp. 114-115.
[195]*Ibid,* p. 116.
[196]*Ibid,* p. 117.

> Pakistan. We are opposed to the idea of limiting the right of missionary activities of Islam within any particular area."[197]

Jami'yat's objectives involved the preservation and promulgation of *shariah* in the Indian sub-continent. Though, shariah in this regard was limited to mere application of the Islamic personal law into the private lives of Muslims. It was suspicious that the Western educated leadership of the League would not allow it to enforce even this abridged version of s*hariah* and would impose their modernist alterations and naturalist interpretations in its proposed Muslim state. They felt more secure in India than in Pakistan. Although, some of the league-leaders have given the assurance that Pakistan would be based upon the Qur'an and Sunnah, yet Jinnah's statements ran contrary to it.[198] He declared his secular policy unequivocally:

> "You may belong to any religion or caste or creed- that has nothing to do with the business of the State. - - - You will find that in course of time Hindus would cease to be Hindus and Muslims would cease to be Muslims, not in the religious sense, because that is the personal faith of each individual, but in the political sense as citizens of the State."[199]

The *'ulama* belonging to Jamaiyat were aware of the fact. Therefore, they were unwilling to support a sheer worldly scheme that, in their view, has no relevance to Islam, rather, harmful in terms of the future of Islam and Muslims in Hindu-India.

---

[197]Ibid,

[198]Faruqi, pp. 118-120.

[199]*Ibid*, p. 121.

Khudai Khidmatgar

Another close ally of Congress among the Muslim organisations was *Khudai Khidmatgar* founded by Khan Abdul Ghaffar Khan, a Pakhtoon popularly known as *Sarhadi Gandhi*, in 1920s, with a strong belief in Gandhi ji's notion of non-violence. He regarded it as the true religion of the Prophet. He addressed his fellow men:

> "I am going to give you such a weapon that the police and the army would not be able to stand against it. It is the weapon of the Prophet, but you are not aware of it. That weapon is patience and righteousness. No power on earth can stand against it."

The organisation recruited over 100,000 members and became legendary less for their peaceful opposition but more for their suffering in the hands of the British-controlled police and army. On April 23, 1930, a crowd of *Khudai Khidmatgar*s gathered in Qissa Khwani Bazaar of Peshawar to protest against the arrest of their leader. The British opened fire on the unarmed crowd, killing an estimated 200-250 *Khudai Khidmatgars.*

Through political organisation, strikes, and non-violent opposition, the *Khudai Khidmatgars* were able to achieve some foothold and came to dominate the politics of the North West Frontier Province. Dr. Khan Abdul Jabbar Khan, a brother of Khan Ghaffar Khan, led the political wing of the movement, and had been the Chief Minister of the province from the late 1920s to 1947 when his government was dismissed by Jinnah for his pro-Indian bent of mind.

Ghaffar Khan strongly opposed the partition of India. As the leader of Pakhtuns he was more comfortable in India than Pakistan. Hence, he was targeted as anti-Muslim and attacked, in 1946, by fellow Muslims leading to his hospitalisation at Peshawar. He had been always labelled as anti-Pakistani and kept under house arrest by all successive Pakistani governments till his death in 1985.

Muslim League and Muslim Nationalism

On the other hand, the Muslim League, founded in 1906,[200] comprising largely of Aligarh based English-educated Muslim elite,[201] under the leadership of Muhammad Ali Jinnah, presented its 'Two Nation theory' which insisted that the Muslims of the Indian subcontinent were a separate nation, distinct from the Hindus and other communities by any definition of a nation and by all canons of international law. They have, in Jinnah's words, their own distinctive culture and civilisation, language and literature, art and architecture, names and nomenclature, sense of value and proportion, legal laws and moral codes, customs and calendar, history and traditions, aptitudes and ambitions. Hence, they require a separate and sovereign homeland consisting of the Muslim majority areas of the subcontinent.

The League under the leadership of Muhammad Ali Jinnah launched, in 1940, a massive Pakistan Movement to pressurise the British to divide India into two sovereign states; one for Hindus and other for Muslims, before leaving the country. This demand reflected the sentiments of middle class Muslims who, being backward in all spheres, were frightened with their Hindu counterparts in an independent India. It was the outcome of the mixed feeling of fear and pride; fear of all sorts and the pride of

---

200Zakaria, p. 110.

201It is noteworthy that entire western educated Muslim intelligentsia was not behind the demand for Pakistan. A secular minded group, having luminaries such as Muhammad 'Ali Jauhar, Abul Kalam Azad, Zakir Hussain, Muhammad Mujib, 'Abid Hussein in its fold, stood for the composite nationalism. (Aziz Ahmed, p. 194)

being the once unquestioned lords of the subcontinent.

Muslim League raised the cry of 'Islam in danger' to attract the masses. Soon it became a popular goal, in the Muslim-dominated provinces, to be achieved at any cost.[202] Jinnah was ready to sacrifice the twenty million Muslims living as minorities in various parts of India in the interests of the Muslim majority provinces.[203]

Maududi & Concept of Muslim Ummah

Maudūdi, at this juncture, evaluated and analysed all these prevailing notions but none could satisfy his mind that was in search of a truly Islamic concept. He, in his initial stage, attracted towards nationalism and, later for a while, communal separatism. However, none among these concepts could have any profound and permanent influence upon his mind. He, dismayed with all these, retrieved towards the original sources of Islam. After a deep and profound critical and analytical study, he was able to present a theory of his own that can be regarded as 'the state-centred theory of the Islam'. Consequent to his preoccupation with the political subjects, like *jihad*, he could not retain his theory unadulterated by the exigencies of his milieu.

Maudūdi had a firm and unshakeable faith upon the Universality, Eternity, and Comprehensiveness of the Islam. He was not to discard or amend any part of the Islam, how minute it might be. In his view, Islam presents the most balanced scheme of life and social justice. No other religion provides the opportunities for development of personality and leads him towards the real

---

[202]*Ibid,* pp. 94-95.
[203]*Ibid,* p. 112.

liberty.[204] For him, there was nothing in the Qur'ãn and the Sunnah that requires alteration or modification.[205] However, his attitude towards the *ijma', qiyas,* and *istihsan* was flexible and in his view, they can be reviewed to meet the exigencies of the age by way of *tawil,* i.e. exegesis of Qur'ãn and Sunnah.206 However, his exegeses of the Qur'ãn were so literalist that there was virtually a little scope for any modernist alteration.

His attitude towards the science and the West was unrepentant and unapologetic, rather assertive and uncompromising. Hence, he could attract the university educated Muslim youth towards his writings and successfully retrieve them to Islam. He condemned Sir Syed's naturalistic interpretation of the Qur'ãn and his modernistic adventurism with Qur'ãnic Angelology, Demonology, Eschatology and Cosmology. He sternly adhered to the traditional interpretations in this regard. In his view, the dictums of science changes so frequently that it would be imprudent to rely upon them, while as the West was baseless altogether. Hence, it is not the Islam that has to be adjusted in accordance with science or the West but, rather, the science and the West itself has to be modified according to the Islam.

In *'Aqaed* he followed the *'Asharites* and in jurisprudence the *Hanafites*. However, he, following the *Waliullahi* tradition never insisted upon following of a specific school or any of the four schools of jurisprudence. In his view, no one except the Prophets was impeccable, hence, no one was beyond criticism and the doors

---

[204]Maudūdi, *Masla-e Qaumiat,* Markazi Maktaba Islami, New Delhi, 1994, pp. 18-19., Hence, *Qaumiyat.*

[205]Abul A'la Maudūdi, ed. Khursid Ahmed, *Islami Riyasat,* Islamic Book Foundation, New Delhi, 1999, pp. 300-301., Hence, *Islami Riyasat.*

[206]*Ibid,* pp. 453-461.

of *Ijtihad* were still open.207 Nevertheless, he did not favour those who try to discard the jurisprudence altogether and strive to evolve their own without sufficient knowledge.208 On the contrary, he paid tribute to the founders of all the traditional schools of jurisprudence.

He condemned the tendency to identify or assimilate Islam with the prevalent concepts or ideologies. For him, Islam has its own identity; it is a way of life and a complete system in itself; hence, it cannot be assimilated or identified with Socialism or Capitalism, Democracy or Aristocracy. Thus, he rejected the Islamic Socialism of Maulana Obaidullah Sindhi, Iqbāl and Hifz al-Rahman Sihwarwi. He envisaged Islam as a comprehensive religion that deals as much with politics as with worship rituals. He, like Iqbāl, considered Islam as a creed, ethical code, plus a polity. He refused to restrict Islam to a mere set of rites and rituals, or personal laws. He always considered temporal power as the basic necessity of Islam. In his view, Islam is a universal religion that is not a possession of any particular race or region, colour or caste, rather a missionary religion that aims to expand itself through propagation.

He, like Iqbāl, al-Afghani and Hasan al-Banna, was very critical and a staunch opponent of modern nationalism.[209] For him, as pointed out by Charles J. Adams, 'Islam is the polar opposite of Nationalism and all that nationalism stands for'.[210] Where there is

---

[207]Abu Tariq, *Maulana Maudūdi kay Interview*, Markazi Maktaba Islami, New Delhi, 1994, p. 34. Hence, Abu Tariq.

[208]*Islami Riyasat*, p. 444.

[209]Maudūdi quotes the popular couplet of Iqbāl that 'it's(nationalism's) very dress is the shroud of the religion'. *Islami Riyasat,* p. 238.

[210]Charles J. Adams, "Mawdudi and the Islamic State", in John L. Esposito, ed. *Voices of Resurgent Islam,* p.103., Hence, Adams.

Islam there is no place for nationalism and vice versa.[211] Nationalism, Maudūdi writes, is a religion in itself. It is an opponent of Divine religions. It seeks all those spheres of human life that, indeed, belong to realm of religion.[212]

In his view, nationalism is not a novel concept but a primitive one and essentially a term of ignorance. It has been in vogue since the very existence of the civilisation.[213] Greek, Roman, Iranian and Jewish nationalisms which prevailed three thousand years earlier were best examples of such kind.[214]

According to Maudūdi, the basic problem with regard to the application of the nationalism was that it could not liberate itself from the shackles of racial and tribal prejudices. Since its very beginning, it has been relied upon the racial, linguistic, geographical and such other elements. Common descent or unity of race has been an integral part of this concept. It was, for him, the outcome of the *'Asbia-e Jāhilia,* the prejudices of ignorance.[215]

Maudūdi regards the *'Asbiah,* prejudice, as the second biggest enemy of Islam after polytheism. For him, it has been a curse for humanity as it divides the people into innumerable sections that can exterminate each other but cannot be amalgamated into each other. It develops such a hatred and antagonism in one nation against the other. This, Maudūdi says, cannot be resolved by any mean. Hence, these nations have been in a state of continuous conflict against each other. *Asbiah,* says Maudūdi, has been the main cause behind all injustice, oppression and despotism. It has been the reason behind the wars among the Arab tribes for thousands of years and

---

[211]*Qaumiyat,* pp. 109-111.
[212]*Ibid,* p. 136.
[213]*Islami Riyasat*, p. 245., see also, *Qaumiat*, p. 7.
[214]*Ibid,* p. 209., see also *Qaumiat*, p. 10.
[215]*Ibid,* p. 222., see also *Qaumiat*, p.11.

even today it has been the basic factor behind all the evils, such as war between different countries, colonial oppression and imperial exploitations. He contends that Islam came to exterminate all such prejudices.216

In contrast to the above, writes Maudūdi, Islam considers the entire humanity as one and equal because it is created by a single couple.[217] He quotes the Qur'ãn:

> "O mankind! Reverence your Guardian-Lord, who created you from a single Person, created, of like nature, his mate, and from them twain scattered (like seeds) countless men and women; fear Allah, through Whom ye demand your mutual (rights), and (reverence) the wombs (that bore you): for Allah ever watches over you".[218]
>
> "It is He Who hath produced you from a single Person; here is a place of sojourn and a place of departure: We detail Our Signs for people who understand".[219]

Maudūdi, further clarifies by citing yet another verse of the Qur'ãn which says that races and tribes are merely for the purpose of identification and the criterion for honour lies in righteousness and piety:

> "O Mankind! We created you from a single (pair) of a male and a female, and made you into nations and tribes, that ye may know each other (not that ye may despise each other). Verily the most honoured of you in the sight of Allah is (he who is) the most righteous of

---

[216]*Ibid,* pp. 207-211., see also *Qaumiat*, pp. 10-11.
[217]*Ibid,* pp. 216-219.
[218]Qur'ãn, 4:1., see also Abul A'la Maudūdi, *Tafhim al-Qur'ãn*, Zafar Ishaq Ansari, Eng. tr. *Towards Understanding the Qur'ãn*, vol. II. p. 5. Hence *Understanding the Qur'ãn.*
[219]*Ibid,* 6:98., see also, *Understanding the Qur'ãn,* vol. II. p. 258.

> you. And Allah has full Knowledge and is well-acquainted (with all things)".[220]

In brief, Maudūdi argues that Muslims have an identity of their own as an *ummah.* They are not bound together by ties of race, colour, geography, language, political system, mutual interest, economics or even culture but by their commitment to follow the Will of God. Hence, they are distinct from the rest of the nations. Therefore, they cannot form a part of any other nation.[221]

He, based on the above fact, rejected both theories, the composite nation theory as well as Muslim separatism. He, like Iqbal, refused to accept the theological justification presented by Maulana Hussain Ahmed Madani (in his *Muttahidah Qaumiyat aur Islam*) for the composite nation theory that the nations are created by political boundaries. He questioned Madani that 'If it is true, why there are ethnical, cultural and religious conflicts endemic in many states including the European? He blamed Madani of wilful distortions of the Arabic dictionary and even the meaning of the verses of the Qur'an.[222] Similarly, he rejected Maulana Azad's argument that the Covenant of Medina provides the basis to constitute a unified nation with other communities.223 He argued:

> "The Muslims and the Jews of Medina did not form a single nation even after the Prophet had brought about an alliance between them for a short while after his

---

[220]*Ibid,* 49:13.

[221]Maulana Maudūdi again quotes a popular couplet of Iqbāl that 'Don't connotes our nation to the western nations since the constituents of Hashemite Prophet's Nation are distinct, their(West's) unity is based upon the country and descent but yours(Muslim's) unity is depend upon the force of religion'. (*Islami Riyasat,* p. 243)

[222]Ishtiaq Hussain Qureshi, *Ulema in Politics*, Maarif, Karachi 2 ed.1974, pp. 351-352

[223]*Qaumiyat,* pp. 86-89.

migration from Mecca to that city. The guarantee of fundamental rights and the assurance to safeguard Muslim personal law did not ensure continued immunity from non-Muslim influences and corrosion of Muslim entity and culture."[224]

In response to Congress' stance, Maudūdi warns the Muslims that if they accept the composite nation theory they would, in fact, be constrained to accept and manifest the identity of the Hindu majority.225 He also suggests that independence from the British was not worthwhile in itself if the Indian Muslims were to exchange servitude to outsiders for that to the majority within their own country. He writes that from the Islamic point of view there was no difference between paramountcy of Indians or British over India, both were equally *shirk*. Hence, he argues that the Muslims shall not participate in the freedom struggle under Congress.[226]

But, simultaneously, Maudūdi repudiated the idea of separate state for Muslims. He also rejected the multi-national Pan-Islamism of Iqbāl, 'Obaidullah Sindhi and such others. He stated that in Islam there is no such concept of geographical and territorial homeland for Muslims.[227] Hence, Maudūdi, with the same vigour, also opposed the Pakistan Movement. He considered it on a par with nationalism. He presented his own two-nation theory that is unique in the sense that it is based upon the Islam and quite different from that of Muslim League. League's theory considers the Muslims of Indian subcontinent as a separate nation distinct

---

[224]Ishtiaq Hussain Qureshi, *Op. cit.*
[225]*Qaumiat*, pp. 98-99.
[226] Maudūdi, *Islami Siyasat*, part III, *Musalman aur Mawjūdah Siyasi Kashmakash*, Markazi Maktaba Islami, Delhi, 1996, p. 44., Hence, *Siyasi Kashmakash.*
[227]*Qaumiat*, pp. 73-82.

from the rest of Indians, on one hand, and the Muslims of the world, on the other. In contrast to this, Maudūdi's two-nation theory agrees with the first part of League's theory but bluntly repudiates the second. In brief, Maudūdi identifies Muslims as distinct from non-Muslims but he was not ready to form a separate homeland for them on the basis of this distinction. On the contrary, he wish to bring all the non-Muslims into the fold of Islam and thereby establish a universal Islamic state.

Maudūdi says, Islam recognises only two categories, or nations in the modern terminology, namely one of the believers and the other of non-believers. All those who profess faith belong to the Muslim *ummah* and all those who refuse, do not belong to it. It does not make any difference that which region or race they belong to. Hence, there cannot be Indian Muslims, Syrian Muslims etc.228 He quotes the Qur'ãn:

> "There is for you an excellent example (to follow) in Abraham and those with him, when they said to their people: "We are clear of you and of whatever ye worship besides Allah: we have rejected you, and there has arisen, between us and you, enmity and hatred forever, unless ye believe in Allah and Him alone"".[229]
>
> "O ye who believe! take not for protectors your fathers and your brothers if they love infidelity above Faith: if any of you do so, they do wrong".[230]

On this basis, writes Maudūdi, Islam presents its own and unique concept of *ummah* that transcends all those evils that are inherent in the ancient as well as modern nationalism. It assimilates all those who believe in Omnipotence of God Almighty and finality

---

[228]*Islami Riyasat*, pp. 224-227., see also *Qaumiat*, p. 163.
[229]*Qur'ãn*, 60:4., see also, *Tafhim*, vol. V. pp. 428-431.
[230]*Ibid,* 9:23., see also, *Understanding the Qur'ãn*, vol. III. p.198.

of the Prophethood of Muhammad. Faith is the basic cohesive and the only unifying factor amidst the diversity of racial, linguistic, geographical factors. It was based upon the fraternity of creed.231 Moreover, *ummah,* as presented by Maudūdi, was a liquid form of unity because any one can become a member of this entity by just professing and adopting certain faith and their commitment to follow the will of God in their lives.232 Further, it provides the strongest and most cohesive relationship among its members. It declares all the members of the *ummah* as brothers regardless of their previous affiliations. The Qur'ãn says:

> "Thus have We made of you an *ummat* justly balanced, that ye might be witnesses over the nations, and the Messenger a witness over yourselves; and we appointed the *Qibla* to which thou wast used, only to test those who followed the Messenger from those who would turn on their heels (from the Faith)".[233]

Maudūdi further explains the inconsistency of the concept of nationalism to Islam. He states that the Qur'ãn never envisages the Arabic synonyms, like *Qaumiyyah, Sho'eb* etc., to designate Muslims, rather it prefers to call them *Hizb,* or *Ummah* i.e. party. Similarly, the Prophet uses *Jama'at*, that too means party, to denote the Muslim community.234 He quotes the following Qur'ãnic verses:

> "The evil one has got the better of them: so he has made them lose the remembrance of Allah. They are the *Hizb* (Party) of the evil one. Truly, it is the party of the evil one that will perish!".[235]

---

[231]*Islami Riyasat,* pp. 224-225.
[232]*Ibid,* pp.224-225.
[233]*Qur'ãn,* 2:143., see also, *Understanding the Qur'ãn,* vol. I. p. 120.
[234]*Islami Riyasat*, pp. 245-250., see also *Qaumiat*, pp. 161-170.
[235]*Qur'ãn*, 58:19.

"They are the Party of Allah. Truly it is the Party of Allah that will achieve Felicity".[236]

"Thus have We made of you an *ummat* justly balanced, that ye might be witnesses over the nations, and the Messenger a witness over yourselves;"[237]

"Ye are the best *ummat* (Peoples), evolved for mankind, enjoining what is right, forbidding what is wrong, and believing in Allah. If only the People of the Book had Faith, it were best for them: among them are some who have Faith, but most of them are perverted transgressors."[238]

Maudūdi enunciates that *ummat* is the best suitable term for Muslim community that is bound together by their commitment to follow the Will of God in their lives. He elucidates that the basic attribute of a party will be its stern adherence to ideology not to the personalities or members. The principles and ideology of the party will be the criteria to decide the foe or friend; if a member follows its principles he will be regarded as friend and every possible co-operation will be extended unto him. But, whenever he violates the ideological principles he would be branded as an enemy and his membership will be terminated with immediate effect. In contrast to this, the nation will be based upon the common descent; hence, no question of violation ever arises.239

Maudūdi clarifies that though Islam is a party, it cannot associates or merges with any political or social system as it has a totalitarian and comprehensive system of life in itself.[240]

---

[236] *Ibid,* 58:22.

[237] *Ibid,* 2:143., see also, *Understanding the Qur'ãn,* vol. I. p. 120.

[238] *Ibid,* 3:110., see also *Understanding the Qur'ãn*, vol. I. p. 278.

[239] *Qaumiat*, pp.161-162., see also, S*iyasi Kashmakash*, pp. 33-34

[240] *Islami Riyasat*, pp. 257-258.

Maudūdi connotes the degeneration of the Muslim *ummah* with the development of nationhood-tendencies among them. He states that Muslims in the due course of time have forgotten their status of being a party and fashioned as a nation struggling for the betterment in economic, political and social terms. He writes:

> "But, Muslims gradually forget the fact that they are indeed a party, and their nationality is based upon their capacity as a party. This forgetfulness, increasing constantly, reached to the extent that the concept of party vanished completely and has been replaced with the concept of nationality. Muslims at present are mere a nation. A nation on a par with Germans, Japanese or Britons. They have totally forgotten those principles and ideology, which binds them into an *Ummah*; and the mission that organises them into a party".[241]

Maudūdi argues that due to this basic defect Muslims are drifting away from the real Islam. They are also thinking in terms of national interest and national sympathy and for the sake of it they are helping each other even against the principles of Islam. This national sympathy develops a tendency to benefit Muslims on the cost of Islam. Gradually, the material interests of Muslims became more important than the Islamic interests and in course of time, such interests are regarded as Islamic interests. Similarly, Muslim governments are regarded Islamic governments, and so on.[242]

Based on the above points, he argues, that a homeland for the Muslims is something different from the *dar al-Islam.* He disagrees with those who speak merely in terms of political freedom or self-determination for Muslims. Pakistan as envisaged by Jinnah and

---

[241] *Ibid,* pp. 251-252.

[242] *Ibid,* pp. 252-254., see also, *Qaumiat*, pp. 170-176.

Muslim League, says Maudūdi, is un-Islamic, rather would be a pagan state and its rulers would be Pharaohs and Nimrods. To call Pakistan an Islamic state would be as misleading as to call an institution of ignorance, perhaps Aligarh Muslim University, as Islamic university.[243] He repudiates the misconception that once a Muslim nation state is established then it can be gradually changed into an Islamic state.[244] It doesn't mean that he was not interested in establishment of an independent state for the Muslims. In fact, for him, the reigns of the state were essential to follow the Islam in toto, but, according to Maudūdi, the aim of Muslims should not be to form a Nation state for themselves but they must strive for an 'ideological state' on the basis of Islam.[245]

He envisages a Universal State that would be beyond the geographical and racial considerations. His justification for this state has been '*al-ardhu li-llah, al-mulku li-llah,* i.e. the land belongeth to God Almighty, hence, the right to rule belongeth to God Almighty alone. In fact, the need and justification for an Islamic state, for him, follows from the nature of universal order. It is a part of a broad integrated theology which is based upon the Sovereignty of the very Creator of the Universe. In Maudūdi's view, this Sovereignty has been enforced automatically in the physical and natural sphere of life. However, in volitional life, the human beings have physical liberty to acknowledge his sovereignty or refuse to do so, but morally they are bound to acknowledge as they have concluded an agreement with Him on the *Yaom-e Alast.*[246] Islam insists upon the acceptance of His sovereignty that

---

[243]Aziz Ahmed,, p. 214.

[244]*Siyasi Kashmakash*, p.133.

[245]*Ibid,* p. 52.

[246]The day of Covenant. Qur'ãn claims that Almighty drew the souls of all the human beings whom He intended to create until the Day of

implies complete submission in all the spheres of life, including legal and political. Hence, to be a Muslim, one has to surrender his free will to the Will of the Almighty and follow His Commandments namely *shari'ah*, in all matters. In his view, the core of the mission of all the Prophets, from the first descendant Prophet Adam to the last Prophet Muhammad, was to call the humanity towards such a complete submission. Consequently, he identified four sources of the constitution of the Islamic state, established under such as Divine Sovereignty, viz. the Qur'ãn and the Sunnah, the Conventions of the four orthodox caliphs and the Rulings of great jurists of Islam.247

Maudūdi's argument against the composite nation theory, from the Islamic point of view, may be or may not be correct, but his view could not gain popular support because he failed to present an instant and attractive alternative before the Indian Muslims. For the majority of Muslims, his ideological Islamic state seems to be an ideal one but a distant goal that can be achieved through centuries, while they were in a dire need of an immediate solution to their problem of domination by the Hindu majority. Similarly, his proposal of confederation falls short of popular aspirations. It is quite strange that Maudūdi, such a genius, could not grasp the urgency of a political solution for Muslims.

Further, he condemned the pro-independence and pro-Pakistan elements for their stand to achieve independence or Muslim homeland as a first step and then to proceed for the ideal Islamic state. Maudūdi pronounced it as impractical. In fact, that was the only possibility at that moment and later, he also resorted to the

---

Judgment and made them testify. All have taken the oath of allegiance that they would obey and worship Him.

[247] Abul A'la Maudūdi, Eng.tr. & ed. Khurshid Ahmed, *Islamic law and Constitution,* New Delhi, 1986, pp. 203-204.

same. It seems that the personal attributes of the leaders of the movement annoyed him more than the actual idea of Pakistan. His stress over the un-Islamic character of League-leaders suggests the same:

> "There, the meetings continue even during the prayer times and if it stops half-heartedly neither the leaders nor the followers rise to offer *namaz*. In such meetings, no sign of Islamic culture is visible, either in dress, etiquette or manners."[248]

Maudūdi presented his own theory of comprehensive Islam that at once rejected all the above theories. In his view, Islam descended to establish God Almighty's Will all over the earth, hence, acquiring just a piece of land for Muslims was out of context and un-Islamic. Muslims were distinct from Hindus but they were not a nation in western sense of the term; they were rather *Ummah*, i.e. an ideological party; a party with a specific mission, namely propagation of Islam across the globe. To achieve this end, he along with some seventy odd like-minded people, established Jamāt-e-Islami in 1941.

----

[248] *Siyasi Kashmakash*, p. 79.

Conclusion

Beginning from the Quran, one leads to the conclusion that it presents a comprehensive scheme of human life that includes the congregational and political realm too. However, it's true that the instructions in this regard has been very limited to draw an outline of the Islamic polity. In the Quranic scheme of state there is specific and stern stress upon the principle of Divine Sovereignty. It is, no doubt, the focal point of the all the teachings of the Quran. However, it is controversial among the Muslims jurists that whether the sovereignty demands by the Quran is limited merely to the natural field? Or it extends and applies to the volitional sphere too.

The advocates of politics-centered theory of Islam argue that the very words, *Ilah* and *Rabb* used in Arabic to denote the God Almighty includes the sense of 'Leader, Head, Chief or Lord; one whose word is obeyed, and whose supremacy or over-lordship acknowledged, and who has authority to dispose of men or things; the Owner, the Master, and the Superior who possesses the requisite authority and the power to do every thing. Further, the Quranic injunctions claiming the sovereignty, such as 2: 165,[249] 2:252,[250] 6:16,[251] 6:57,[252] 7:172,[253] 10:31,[254] 12:40,[255] 17:42-43,[256]

[249] Yet there are men who take (for worship) others besides Allah, as equal (with Allah): they love them as they should love Allah, but those of Faith are overflowing in their love for Allah. If only the unrighteous could see, behold, they would see the Punishment: that to Allah belongs all power, and Allah will strongly enforce the Punishment. (2: 165)

[250] Knowest thou not that to Allah belongeth the dominion of the heavens

18: 26,[257] 23:83,[258] 23:86,[259] 23:88,[260] 25:2,[261] 43:87,[262] 51:58,[263]

---

and the earth? Besides Him, ye have neither patron nor helper. (2:252)
[251] If Allah touches thee with affliction, none can remove it but He; if He touch thee with happiness, He hath power over all things." He is the Irresistible, (watching) from above over His worshippers; and He is the Wise, Acquainted with all things. (6: 16)
[252] The command rests with none but Allah. He declares the truth and He is the best of judges. (6: 57)
[253] When thy Lord drew forth from the Children of Adam from their loins, their descendants, and made them testify concerning themselves, (saying): "Am I not your Lord (Who cherishes and sustains you)?" They said: "Yea! We do testify!" (This), lest ye should say on the Day of Judgment: "Of this we were never mindful". (7: 172)
[254] Say: "Who is it that sustains you (in life) from the sky and from the earth? Or who is it that has power over hearing and sight? And who is it that brings out the living from the dead and the dead from the living? And who is it that rules and regulates all affairs?" They will soon say, "Allah". Say, "Will ye not then show piety (to Him)?" (10: 31)
[255] The command is for none but Allah's. (12: 40);
[256] Say: if there had been (other) gods with Him, - as they say - behold, they would certainly have sought out a way to the Lord of the Throne! Glory to Him! He is high above all that they say! Exalted and Great (beyond measure)! (17: 42-43);
[257] Say: "Allah knows best how long they stayed: with Him is (the knowledge of) the secrets of the heavens and the earth: how clearly He sees, how finely He hears (everything)! They have no protector other than Him; nor does He share His Command with any person whatsoever. (18: 26)
[258] Say: "To whom belong the earth and all beings therein? (Say) if ye know!"(23: 83);
[259] Say: "Who is the Lord of the seven heavens, and the Lord of the Throne (of Glory) Supreme?" (23: 86);
[260] Say: "Who is it in whose hands is the governance of all things, who protects (all), but is not protected (of any)? (Say) if ye know." (23: 88)

59:23,[264] 62:1,[265] and many more, is so obvious that nothing more would be required to prove it. The concerning verses seem to demand the recognition of His Sovereignty in both, natural as well volitional, spheres from the humanity in unequivocal words. These verses warned the Muslims that they must not accept any others suzerainty over themselves and their life lest they would be polytheists. In fact, in the light of these verses, Omnipotence of God and the Divine Sovereignty are so vitally intertwined that the negation of one amounts the negation of the other *ipso facto*.

Further, the Quran condemns the Jews that, in course of time, they forgotten Allah, and made their leaders and Rabbis as their Gods; and it is a historical fact that the Jews never regarded their leaders as God but they have just accepted their suzerainty in worldly life. It implies that for God regarding some one as Sovereign in political life would be equal to having him as *Ilah*, God. Further, Moses was instructed to approach, at first instance it self, the Emperor of the land with the message from the God to

---

[261] He to Whom belongs the dominion of the heavens and the earth: no son has He begotten, nor has He a partner in His dominion: it is He Who created all things, and ordered them in due proportions. (25: 2);

[262] If thou ask them, Who created them, they will certainly say, Allah: how then are they deluded away (from the Truth)? (43: 87)

[263] For Allah is He Who gives (all) Sustenance, - Lord of Power - steadfast (forever). (51: 58)

[264] Allah is He, than Whom there is no other god; the Sovereign, the Holy One, the Source of Peace (and Perfection), the Guardian of Faith, the Preserver of Safety, the Exalted in Might, the Irresistible, the Supreme: Glory to Allah! (High is He) above the partners they attribute to Him. (59: 23)

[265] Whatever is in the heavens and on earth, doth declare the Praises and Glory of Allah; the Sovereign, the Holy One, the Exalted in Might, the Wise. (62: 1)

accept Later's supremacy.

In response to the objections that 'if the establishment of God's suzerainty is the central theme of Islam why clear-cut scheme of state is not provided in Quran, they rightly pointed out the fact that, it is not the case limited to political issues; even in the matter of basic ritual of Islam namely, *Salat*, the Quran provides only basic outlines, not the complete procedure lest there would not be differences among Muslim Jurists regarding issues like *Rafe Yadain, Fatiha Khalaf ul Imam*, pronouncing *Bismillah* before *Surat ul Fatiha* etc.

The opponents of the political Islam argues that the emphasis of all the above presented Quranic verses are upon Omnipresence of the God Almighty in Universe's natural field; it did not include the political realm as the later is a very trivial thing in the eyes of the God (there are many Quranic verses which declares that this world has no worth in the eyes of God). It is below His stature that He would send hundreds of thousands of Messengers and Prophets just to establish His Kingship on earth or portion of it. In fact, very few, only three of the known Prophets, among these messengers / prophets became kings or rulers. The Quran requires that the human beings regard Him as the Only God and abide themselves voluntarily by His Ordains; it does not imply that the obedience to any body else would harm His suzerain status as long as this obedience would not go against His Ordains. They say that if establishment of His sovereignty would be the sole aim and the central-theme of Islam, Islam would be equated to chaos and bloodshed, instead of peace as the word literally means, as it would strive for overthrowing of the existing regime. Further, when the kingship was offered to the Prophet Mohammad by the Pagans of the Arab he refused it. Moses did not ask the Pharaoh to relinquish his throne; he was just asked to accept the Omnipresence of Allah and to refute his own claim of being god. Joseph was continued as loyal employee of the existing regime even after receiving the status of a prophet. The Prophet Mohammad himself had written many letters to the Kings and Emperors of his times with a message to accept the Omnipresence of God Almighty and Prophet-hood of himself but never asked to relinquish their thrones, or merge their kingdoms to the kingdom of God or regard him as their Sovereign.[266] The Prophet never presented him as king or head of a state. Whenever some pagan approached him his stress was upon spiritual, not upon political; He sent orators of Quran, not Governors to their lands.

In brief, the opponents believe that the temporal authority is not basic and central to Islam, however, some of its manifestations may require it; but, if it could not be accomplished it would not harm the religion of any believer. The religious rituals can also be performed without any theological hindrance. However, complete enforcement of Islam requires the temporal authority. Some of them believe that it comes as the reward for the good deeds of the believers.

Both the above arguments are so strong that it is difficult to negate/favour one or the other. In fact, the truth lies between the lines, as envisaged, to some extent, by Ibn Taimiya. That is to say, though establishment of the Political authority is not the central-theme of Islam, it (Islam) requires the authority in its hands as it aims to shape the entire society according to its own scheme that involves imposition of certain punishments also.

The second question is about the form of government that what would be the system of government? Hierarchical kingship,

---

[266] It is recorded in the history that the Christian King of Ethopia grasped the above mentioned fact and accepted Islam. Nevertheless, he was not asked by the Prophet to merge his kingdom with the state of Medina or relinquish his kingship etc.

dictatorship, democracy or theocracy? Various, some time strange, answers were given by the Muslim jurists. There is little in Quran in this regard. In fact, it left the matter to the choice of the believers and requirements of the circumstance. If one comes to the precedence during period of Prophet and Righteous Caliphs, there are various methods adopted in various situations. Prophets is out of question here as he was designated by the God Himself. Then, one comes across with the installation of Hzt. Abu Bakr to the caliphate. It was astonishingly regarded by some Muslim jurists as 'election by one man' and on this basis the have justified the usurpation of this apex office by their favorites. In fact, this misunderstanding was due to absence of democratic system in practice as well as in precedence. They were accustomed to the kingship only and unaware of democratic principles and practices, hence, they had mistaken 'the proposal' to 'the election'. In fact, the installation of the first caliph was not by one person but by representatives of the people for the People of Medina was regarded by the entire population of the Islamic state as their representatives. In the second instance, the outgoing caliph appointed his successor out of his kith and kin. Though it seems to be arbitrary and undemocratic but in that peculiar situation it expresses the outgoing caliphs understanding of public opinion. It may be equated with British practice of appointing of Prime Minister by the Queen and later ratification / refutation by people's representatives. The third instance represents panel-procedure. In Hzt. Ali's case he had accepted the office in emergency arised due to the murder of the Caliph. Later, when the normalcy restored he asked the public opinion and some of the historian reported that he had avoided important policy decisions before having the public verdict. Further, he announced, as reported by some historians, that no one has the right to hold the office of the caliph unless he has the popular support. Imam Hussain's stand against illegitimate incumbent in the office of Caliphate made the issue quite clear.

It is the reason that Abu Hanfia always extended his support to those who rise against such usurpers.

Nevertheless, it is fact that there are no clear-cut injunctions in Quran in this regard too. Hence, some of the great jurists like Shafa'ee and Ahmed b. Hanbal, whose honesty, integrity and audacity against the established regime has been beyond any doubt and proved practically on several other occasions, had favoured stability to legitimacy and declared rebellion against even an usurper as a major sin. In this regard also, the middle way between these two extremes is the true path. In other words, if there is a hope of success rebellion against an illegitimate ruler would be the correct option; but, if there is no iota of hope, rebellion would be equal to suicide, hence, not permissible.

There is another controversy with regard to the qualifications of the caliph namely whether the Qureishite descend is a pre-requisite or not? The majority of the Sunni jurists inclined towards the positive answer. There is nothing in Quran in this regard, the advocates of this view present certain traditions from the Prophet. However, in the light of general tendency of the Islamic political teachings that are more or less democratic it seems that the instructions of the Prophet mentioned in traditions were limited to that period due to conditions prevailed in that area during those days. It would be absurd from the Islam, that pronounce that piety is the criteria to decide preference, that it would instruct its followers in China or Alaska, if they reached to a decisive position, to wait and remain without a leader until a Qureishite from the distant lands of Arabia reached to them and accepted their lead.

Not only the system of government in Islamic lands began to be corrupted by the end of the era of four Righteous Caliphs, the opportunist elements among the Muslims started to pollute even the Islamic political theory by interpreting it in their favour. In fact, the seeds were sown during the battles of Camels and Rows when one faction tried to interpret the Prophet's traditions in a novel way.[267] Later, several of Muslims jurists, save few honest ones, follow the suit and tried their level best to present a justification for their Master's misdeeds[268] or for their own office.[269] Hence, it is appropriate to call such opportunist's views, rather as Muslim theory and it is absurd to judge the Islamic Political system based on their opinion.

---

267 There was a tradition popular among the Companions that the Prophet on some occasion propheced that an evil-going faction would kill Ibn Jarrah. Ibn Jarrah in the battle was killed by Hzt. Muawiya's faction. Due to the widest popularity of the above tradition they were not in a position to deny or reject the tradition as fabricated. Hence, they said that the real Murderes of b. Jarrah was those who brought him to the battle-field.

268 Al Mawardi to Justify Abbasid regime, Al Ghazali to Seljuk Sultans,

269 Tusi to provide a theoretical basis for Vizierite as he was Vizier.

www.ingramcontent.com/pod-product-compliance
Ingram Content Group UK Ltd.
Pitfield, Milton Keynes, MK11 3LW, UK
UKHW020128250726
13967UKWH00002B/535